Love Had a Compass

ROBERT LAX

Edited by James J. Uebbing

Grove Press
NEW YORK

Love Had a Compass

Journals and Poetry

FIRST EDITION
Published simultaneously in Canada
Printed in the United States of America

Library of Congress Cataloging-in-Publication Data
Lax, Robert.
    Love had a compass: journals and poetry / Robert Lax: edited by
James J. Uebbing. — 1st ed.
        p.   cm.
    ISBN 0-8021-1587-X
    I. Uebbing, James J.   II. Title.
PS3523.A972L6   1996
811'54—dc20   96-1255

Design by Laura Hammond Hough

Grove Press
841 Broadway
New York, NY 10003

10 9 8 7 6 5 4 3 2 1

Editor's Acknowledgments

ANYONE WHO VALUES the work of Robert Lax must first of all acknowledge a tremendous debt to Bernard Moosbrugger of Pendo Verlag, whose books have almost single-handedly kept Lax in the public eye for the last twenty years, and who has very kindly permitted us to reprint many of the works in this volume.

I am also extremely grateful to Alice Quinn of the *New Yorker*, who encouraged my interest in this project from the start, and to Stephen Koch and Diana Trilling, who provided much useful advice along the way.

Of the many others whose opinions and assistance I relied upon, I wish especially to acknowledge the following: Marcia and Jack Kelly, Paul Spaeth, Bernard Crystal, Donald Ambrose, Julie Nichols, Mimi Munson, Elizabeth Hollander, Fredrik Stanton, and Karen Zusman.

Morgan Entrekin is naturally to be commended for envisioning this work, as are Carla Lalli and everyone else at Grove who managed to carry it through each step of its production.

Contents

Introduction

ROBERT LAX is not well known in this country. As a poet he enjoys a considerably larger audience in Europe than in his native America, and even in Europe his status as a cult figure is obscure. Obscurity, in an elderly artist who has devoted a lifetime to his art, can indicate a good deal; there is the obscurity of the renegade, the pariah, and the failure. There is the obscurity of the timid and the obscurity of the self-assured. The obscurity of those, like Lax, who have simply chosen to be obscure is always to some degree a provocation, a story that calls attention to itself but allows few lessons to be drawn.

Those who have read Thomas Merton will know that Lax was part of Merton's Columbia circle: they will recall him as the shyest, quietest, and least self-conscious of Merton's overly articulate classmates, the one he describes in *The Seven Storey Mountain* as a "potential prophet, but without rage." Rage would certainly have been an issue at hand: social and political turmoil such as that suffered during the Depression and prewar years does not, as a rule, lend much support to the growth of the inner life, but Merton and Lax managed at Columbia not only to avoid the most unlovable moral responses to what Auden would later christen "that low, dishonest decade" but also to find a circle of friends who felt as perversely thrilled by, and estranged from, the contemporary world as they did themselves. Ad Reinhardt, Edward Rice, Robert Giroux, and John Berryman are the best known of these today. Merton and Lax, almost from the start, were the closest.

The fame that Merton was to achieve through his autobiography, his later writings as a Trappist monk and hermit, and the bizarre circumstances of his accidental death in Bangkok in 1968 have made his story familiar, if not widespread, among contemporary Americans. Lax is a different case altogether. Whereas Merton found that his vocation as a Christian and a writer could only find expression within a world whose boundaries were drawn not merely by the Church but by the Abbey of Our Lady of Gethsemani in the Kentucky hills, Lax spent the better part of his life as rootless and expectant as a beggar. Born in Olean, a town in western New York State, he stayed on in Manhattan for some years after he left Columbia but then began a long period of wandering, moving to New London, to North Carolina, to California and Canada. Lax wrote continuously from his college days on, but it is too simple to say of him that he has always been a writer. He wrote for the *New Yorker*, *Time*, and Hollywood; he also went on the road with a circus, taught philosophy, coached boxers (without ever having boxed), and lived in a settlement house in Harlem. He eventually left America altogether in the late 1950s and has returned only infrequently and briefly. His main concern in leaving the States was to find someplace "quiet and inexpensive," and he finally settled on the Greek island of Patmos, where he lives today.

Nowadays Patmos is neither quiet nor cheap, but when Lax arrived it hadn't even a proper harbor and could barely sustain one small hotel. It is a rocky place, mountainous and extremely dry. Nearer to Turkey than to the Greek mainland, it is remote but far from desolate and has been a center of pilgrimage at least since the eleventh century, when the Monastery of St. John was built hard by the cave where the Beloved Desciple, "in exile for the Word of God," wrote his Revelation. The monastery still dominates the island physically and imparts a peculiar tone to the place. Just beneath its ramparts, the old hill town of Chora looks down across the entire island; farther below, the shabbier port town of Skala stretches out against the waterfront. Lax lives in Skala.

Quite a number of people visit Patmos to visit Lax. Especially during the summer, there is a small gathering of them—writers, students, fiancés—most evenings at his little house overlooking the bay. This was how I first visited him in 1991. His verse had impressed me with its strangeness and restraint, and among my own friends at Columbia, stories circulated, some fifty years past Lax's tenure, of the unknown poet who had fallen off the edge of the map somewhere in the Aegean. Poets always generate rumors and fantasies, and with Lax these generally reduced themselves to a kind of consensus that the man was a saint. Or, at least, a hermit.

He may be either or both, but these terms would need to be broken in a good deal before they fit.

Biography, to a large extent, is the explication of motive, and motives ought not to be guessed at too readily. It is not my intention here to provide a biography of Robert Lax. The solitary nature of his present life abroad, and the apparent restlessness of the years that led up to it, could suggest a good deal about him—from self-indulgence to outright misanthropy—that would be at once misleading and beside the point. Lax is not a recluse. Neither has he much in common with the many poor souls—from Paris to Patmos to Prague—who coddle their indolence abroad as expatriates. However vague the pattern of Lax's life may appear, it cannot be missed entirely.

It is important to understand this. All the more so because Lax himself would be the last to insist upon it. Writers in general are loath to work out any equation of their lives, to supply a concordance that would match the elements of their experience to the form of their art, and who could ask otherwise? That is the job of their writing alone. But life, all life, becomes a narrative at some point, and a narrative needs to be told. Lax will tell you that he first visited Patmos because there was a picture of St. John on the wall of his room in Marseille. He lived in that room (in a cheap hotel) for months, and in the evening the very last rays of the sun would highlight this portrayal of the Apostle, busily writing in the Cave of the Apocalypse. A simple response to a simple moment. Simple matters have formed the shape of Lax's life—a simplicity that is real enough to be disarming at first sight.

Marseille itself is a case in point. In 1951 Lax traveled there by a roundabout course and spent some months or years—accounts vary—living among the layabouts and drifters of the old port. At thirty-six Lax had become used to roundabout courses, as had his friends, who knew better than to search out his plans too carefully. He had told them that in Marseille he hoped to write some poems and "get to know poor folks."

Ostensibly, the idea was to establish some sort of hospice for the poor similar to Friendship House in New York, where he had worked under the tutelage of its foundress, Catherine Doherty. It was an eminently practical scheme that, unsurprisingly, came to little. At Friendship House, Lax had become famous for his inability to wash floors with the right end of a mop, and in Marseille he spent several days in a hotel before he realized that it was, in fact, a brothel. As things turned out, he succeeded in a small way: he lived among the poor as a poor man himself and became the center of a small group that met haphazardly for meals in his room at the Hôtel du Calais. For the most part, however, Marseille was an exercise in solitude rather than charity.

Perhaps this was what Lax himself had hoped for: certainly it would appear to have been precisely what he needed. The *fuga mundi* that carried him from America to Marseille to Greece took place just as Lax was developing and settling into a newer and far more mature poetic voice, and there is every indication that what carried him abroad was not so much ennui or wanderlust as a profound inner need that he did not fully understand himself. The arch humor of his earlier verse—the *Fables*, for example, which had relied heavily on wordplay and comedy—was giving way to something quieter and less accessible, works whose center of gravity was more deeply internal and extremely subtle. The most distinctive features of Lax's style—the short lines of verse arranged in long columns, the deadpan narration, the highly abstract imagery—began to take shape around this time.

Marseille appears to have been a crucial force in this shift, and not simply through the happenstance of timing. When Lax made the decision to move abroad, he saw the city as a sinister zone. He had visited it years before while still a student and claims to have been so unnerved by the place—specifically, by a dark café near the old port whose silent customers seemed ghoulish and malign to him in the evening shadows—that he turned and left within hours of his arrival. When Lax chose to leave America, then, it was not his idea to find someplace congenial but to return to someplace strange. It was another of the intimations by which he guided himself.

The most important thing to come out of Lax's time in Marseille was *Port City*, a long verse narrative of his experience there. *Port City*, like *The Circus of the Sun*, is a poem of impressions and declamations: it exemplifies the metaphorical restraint to be found in most of Lax's work, the unwillingness to use words as allusions or indicators. When Lax avers that

> *i had*
> *been coming*
> *toward that*
> *city*
> *since*
> *the beginning*
> *of time*
>
> *i had*
> *been coming*
> *toward*
> *that city*
> *and singing*
> *that city's*
> *song*

it is about as rhetorical as he will get, but even the rhetoric here encloses simple descriptive elements—the "song of the city," which is, after all, what Lax composes.

The impressionistic sequences are just as straightforward:

> *the stone quay*
> *and the sound*
> *of the waters*
>
> *nets stretched*
> *from the mast*
> *to the bow*
>
> *the silverbellied*
> *fish*
> *on racks*
> *and*
> *in baskets*
>
> *the blackhaired*
> *fisherwoman*
> *and her pale son*
>
> *wrinkled forehead*
> *and flashing smile*

Here the images are provided simply and direct, with few of the (real or implied) comparisons that a poetic voice will always contain. The austerity of this style is not merely verbal: the visual arrangement of the lines into "ladders" of verse serves to highlight the elements contained therein, so as to impress their importance upon us. This insistence upon patience, upon attention to trivialities is not an incidental element of design, for simplicity—its centrality as a human virtue and the necessity of its cultivation—is at the heart of Lax's achievement as a poet and a man.

Here, too, the contrast with Merton is of some note. Like Merton, Lax converted to Catholicism as a young man and—although it would be hard to describe him as a "Catholic poet" in the sense that one applies this term to Hopkins, Claudel, or even David Jones—his early verse, like Merton's, clearly shows the power that the Church held over his imagination. For Lax, however, the doctrinal and aesthetic elements of Catholicism do not become a part of his craft: although there is an unmistakably religious framework surrounding such poems as "Jerusalem," for example, one would look through Lax in vain for something as overtly Catholic as the rhetoric and imagery of the English mystics (used to such good effect by Eliot in his *Four Quartets*) or the High Church nostalgia of the young Robert Lowell. In Lax's work Christianity does not intrude itself as either a social or a cultural force, and since (in literary terms) this is practically the only existence it has been granted in our day, it is likely that we may overlook it altogether.

It is the core of his work all the same, and as it provides the only coherent context in which Lax can be read, we ignore it at our peril. In *The Circus of the Sun*, Lax supplies a genealogy for the whole of his art when he improvises on the prologue of St. John's Gospel:

> And in the beginning was love. Love made a sphere:
> all things grew within it; the sphere then encompassed
> beginnings and endings, beginning and end. Love
> had a compass whose whirling dance traced out a
> sphere of love in the void: in the center thereof
> rose a fountain.

Here we are given not the voice of God but the vision of him; the voice belongs to Lax, who stands in the guise not so much of a creator as of a witness. This reticence of tone is typical, quite distinctive, and central to his work. It suggests an aesthetic sensibility somewhat at odds with the cult of the ego that still prevails among writers in our day and hints, in its lack of personality, at literary ambitions quite distinct from self-expression.

It is thus, for many reasons, impossible to consider Lax in strictly literary terms—as one might Wallace Stevens, say, or Geoffrey Hill. The usual interplay between life and art, by which much of what we consider poetic form is created, does not appear in evidence. Lax's work generally takes the form either of transparent narratives—such as *Port City*—that do not attempt to disguise themselves as anything other than verse chronicles of actual events, or of opaque abstractions that give no external display of personality whatsoever.

This is not a minor difference of style, still less an accidental reflection of the poet's temperament. There is a clear intent to Lax's simplicity, and if this is not understood, the work itself will most likely come across as bland and noncommittal. In reality, almost everything that Lax has written since 1960 contains and forms a vast interior architecture that is itself as self-conscious and pointed as it is unobtrusive.

Lax is a poet who does not wish to surprise. He makes very little use of metaphor, and much of his work is almost devoid of imagery as well. The concrete poems are the best illustration of this: something as abstract as

black
black

white
white

red
red

blue
blue

is obviously not attempting to work against the reader's sentiment, and it cannot operate against the reader's intelligence either. As unspecific as it is—and this is in many ways typical of Lax—it can barely even work on the level of suggestion, since a color could suggest various and dissimilar things.

With Lax it is necessary to put aside the very notion of interpretation, the expectation—so basic to us that it is barely recognizable as a strategy—that an author's art will by its nature be linear and syllogistic. We have long since become used to a poetry and a literature that make small claims on the understanding, and it did not take the modernists to break our confidence in the ability of words to correspond with our interior and concrete realities in any exact way. It is less apparent, however, that those who read and write poetry today feel that the present situation calls for any diminishment in the authority of the poet. If anything, the cult of personality seems to flourish under the current circumstances, in which the assertion of the self and the self's desires has become nearly the whole object and soul of poetry.

The example of Robert Lax is bound to prove unsettling to anyone whose sensibilities have been formed along these lines, because his approach is frankly antithetical to such an elevation of personality. *Port City* will suggest a great deal about its author, as will *The Circus of the Sun*, but in these works it is not possible to establish a strict equation of the author with the poet. This cannot be an accident of design. Lax is no less of a spectator than we are: the jugglers and the con men and the shrine of Notre-Dame de la Garde are as unfamiliar to him as they are to us, and while he is far from indifferent to them, there is no real attempt on his part to induce his response in his audience. Indeed, his own response is itself either invisible to us or offered with a reticence that makes few demands upon our credulity. Even the "interior" sequences of *Port City*, such as the magnificent final passage in which Lax declares

> *that all*
> *indeed*
> *was real*
>
> *all had*
> *history*
> *and a*
> *name*

(as though
the moment
had been
rapt beyond
itself
and was eternal
while it
moved
in time)

i saw
each object
then in
its relation
(to a
timeless
being)

and my
heart
sang
(but kept
its deepest
peace)

are offered almost as an aside, and are kept so clearly distinct from the main body of the work that they seem almost to arise from some other source than the events and people that constitute the poem.

And perhaps they do. In the world of Robert Lax cause and effect are murky concepts, hardly nonexistent but not ubiquitous and somehow beside the point in the end. The elements of his art are the elements of the created world: the sea and the men and the animals and the light. Like every artist he makes his use of them, but unlike most he acknowledges that they do not belong to him. They find their origin elsewhere. It is in this respect that Lax must be acknowledged as a religious man, insofar as for him artistic creation is not a ransacking of the visible world or an assertion of some unfettered consciousness so much as it is a participation in a process that was already in motion long before he arrived on the scene.

In his *Autobiography*, Mark Van Doren wrote of Lax that "his chief woe . . . was that he could not state his bliss: his love of the world and of all things, all persons in it. He continues to try." Certainly this is borne out in his verse, and it will be apparent to anyone who has read Lax that Van Doren was able, with a clarity and directness that seem to be the special preserve of teachers, to touch upon the real drama that his old student had begun to enact. It has been enacted obscurely and quietly in a variety of out-of-the-way locales, but it has continued and continues to this day.

JAMES J. UEBBING
New York
November 25, 1995

Occasional Poems

Zoo Sign

At your peril
Feed the squirrel.
Nature is a wolf.

Angry dove
From the branches
Plunges.

Grass will pierce the foot.

Grass will pierce
The angry pigeon.

Lake will swallow
The snarling duck.

Better
Leash the setter
Tighter.

Nature is a wolf.

. . .

Jerusalem

reading of lovely Jerusalem,
lovely, ruined Jerusalem.

we are brought to the port
where the boats in line are
and the high tower on the hill
and the prows starting again
into the mist.

for we must seek
by going down,
down into the city
for our song.
deep into the city
for our peace.
for it is there
that peace lies
folded
like a pool.

there we shall seek:
it is from there
she'll flower.

for lovely, ruined Jerusalem,
lovely, sad Jerusalem
lies furled
under the cities
of light.

for we are only
going down,
only descending
by this song
to where the cities
gleam in darkness,

or curled like roots
sit waiting
at the undiscovered
pool.

what pressure
thrusts us up
as we descend?

pressure of
the city's singing,

pressure of
the song
she hath withheld.

hath long withheld.

for none
would hear
her.

. . .

Andalusian Proverb

rooster
rooster
rooster

rooster
with your
head cut
off:

what
are you
thinking
now,

you rooster,
what are you
thinking now
of the bloody
morning?

. . .

in me
in me
in me

is the
watcher

in me
in me
in me

is the
watcher

in me
is the
watcher

in me
is the
watcher

in me
in me
in me

is the
watcher

. . .

every
night
in the
world

is a
night

in the
hospital

. . .

the port
was longing

the port
was longing

not for
this ship

not for
that ship

not for
this ship

not for
that ship

the port
was longing

the port
was longing

not for
this sea

not for
that sea

not for
this sea

not for
that sea

the port
was longing

the port
was longing

nor for
this &

not for
that

not for
this &

not for
that

the port
was longing

the port
was longing

nor for
this &

not for
that.

. . .

forms
forms
forms

basic
basic
forms

basic
basic
basic
basic
basic
basic
forms

...

mos
qui
to

said:

live
for
this

mo
ment

the

el
e
phant:

live
for
this

day

mos
qui
to:

get
the
point

of

what

i'm
say
ing

el
e
phant:

or
at
least

get
the
gen
er
al

i
de
a

. . .

Three Concrete
Poems

black	white	black	white
black	white	black	white
white	white	white	black
white	white		black
black	black	black	white
black	black	black	
white		white	
white			

. . .

black	red	black	black
black	black	black	black
white	blue	white	white
white	white		white
red	white	red	red
red	black	red	
blue	red	blue	blue
blue	blue		

. . .

red	red	black	red
red	red	black	red
black	black	blue	black
black	black		black
black	black	black	black
black	black	black	black
blue	blue	blue	blue

. . .

Twenty-five
Episodes

i.

he sat
on the edge of his bed
all night

day came
& he continued to sit there

he thought he would never be able
to understand
what had happened

ii.

if i can only
hold my mind together
until
i do this thing
she thought
i'll let it go later
wherever it will run

iii.

she watched the dam growing
and rudolph gaining authority
as it grew

she was gaining authority, too

soon she'd be able to tell him
about her plan

iv.

allowed
the sun to dry her nails
as though
it had
no other work
in the world

v.

otto & wanda's
only
real life
was in bed

outside
they went through the motions

attending concerts
& openings
at the museum

but nothing
they saw or heard
impressed them

vi.

it was only when the dentist
talked to her about life
that she realized she had one

vii.
auntie was one of those people
who are sent
to young girls
at just the right time
to show them how to use
cosmetics
& to pull
their stockings straight

viii.
had spent her life
practicing
to be an old lady

now that she was one
she felt a sense of loss

ix.
all i want
is for my son
to get married

what did you say, mummy?

nothing, son,
nothing at all, i was just
thinking

oh, all right, then,
mumsey

all i want
in the whole bleeding
world

is for my son
to get married

x.

mister eddie
don't live here
no more

his old lady's
gone away
too

he killed
his old man

that grieves
his mother

the two of
them's
tired
of this
neighborhood

xi.

the angel came to him & said

i'm sorry, mac, but
we talked it over
in heaven
& you're going

to have to live
a thousand years

xii.

angel said:

neat, the
way
when he
heard the
thunder

he pulled
the cot
away

from un-
der
the
sky-
light

xiii.
little
carl senn

stood
on
the trestle

he seen
the train
bearin'

down
on
him

but
he
couldn't
do
nothin'

a-
bout
it

xiv.
sloppy talk
keep talking me
that sloppy talk
i like to hear
that sloppy talk
especially
when you talk it
in my ear

xv.
she's got her whole room
hung with pictures
of that man

them together at yachting parties
him with the cup
him playing tennis
& some big diploma
he got from i don't know where

she don't go out anymore at all
just sits in the room
& looks at them things

xvi.
wake up jack
it's 1949

xvii.
the kind of broad-faced
smiling person whose assistant
is always a thin
worried man

xviii.

had
drawn pictures
of him

& made a
statue

in clay

long before
she met him

or even
knew
he
existed

xix.

her daughter ellen
was studying
to be
a bridesmaid
and was continually
dressed
in light blue
tulle

xx.

doris
if i'd wanted
to go in the business
of making dresses
that didn't fit

i'd
have gone
in that business

but i want
to make dresses
that do fit

do you
know what i mean
doris

dresses that
fit

xxi.

you fool,
said the other
pigs

don't you know
they're only
fattening
you

for the slaughter?

what should
i do,
said no. 1

not eat?

xxii.

a dog walked wearily
from one side of the town to the other
saying to himself

"i'll find a cat to chase
today or i'll never leave the house
again"

xxiii.

otto
is dead
now

if he
was here

he'd
imitate

the cat

xxiv.
moth-
er
if
we

don't
move
out
of
blens-
ville

i'll
pro-
bab-
ly

shoot
my-
self,

mo-
ther

do
you
know
that
?

xxv.
oh god,
he said,

perfection!
& rushed
from the room

. . .

Fables

The Man with the Big General Notions

There was a man who said, "Why eat cake when all you want is bread? Why eat frosting when all you want is cake? Why eat cake and frosting when all you want is bread and candy?" The man was accounted very wise, and he thought it was a true account.

When he went to build a house he said, "Why get brick when all you want is HARDNESS?"

> So he got a big rough stone
> And on top of the stone he put a bone
> And on top of the bone he put a box
> And on top of the box he put a bar
> And on top of the bar he put a beam
> And the pile stood five feet high
> And tottered

And then it fell to the ground.

And the man said, "Why should I get cement when all that I need is STICKINESS?"

> So on top of the stone he put some snow
> And on top of the bone he put some glue
> And on top of the box he put some tape
> And on top of the bar he put some gum
> And on top of the pile he put molasses

And the pile stood six feet high.

And the man said, "Why should I shingle a roof when all that I want is SHELTER?"

> So on top of the pile he put a hat
> And next to the hat a big umbrella
> And next to that a manhole cover

And next to that a greening tree
And next to that a turtle shell

And the roof was ten feet wide.

And the man said, "Why should I get a wife when all that I want
is SOMETHING ALIVE?"

So into the house he put a dog
And next to the dog he put a cat
And next to the cat he put a fish
And next to the fish he put a snail
And next to the snail a big baboon

That stood about four feet high.

"And why should I buy a window or bulb when all that I want
is LIGHT?"

So next to the dog he built a fire
And next to the fire he put a glass
And next to the glass he put a jewel
And next to the jewel an electric eel
And next to the eel a forest pool

Which was about twelve feet deep.

And the man said, "Why should I buy a bed when all that I want
is SLEEP?"

So he went to sleep
And the dog went mad
And bit the cat
And the cat ate the fish
And the fish ate the snail
And the tree caught fire
And the molasses ran
And the snow melted
And the hat fell down
And the cover fell in the forest pool
And so did the shell

And so did the gum
And so did the tape
So did the bar
So did the beam
So did the box
So did the bone
So did the glue
So did the stone.

Some man.

Some house.

. . .

Alley Violinist

if you were an alley violinist

and they threw you money
from three windows

and the first note contained
a nickel and said:
when you play, we dance and
sing, signed
a very poor family

and the second one contained
a dime and said:
i like your playing very much,
signed
a sick old lady

and the last one contained
a dollar and said:
beat it,

would you:

stand there and play?

beat it?

walk away playing your fiddle?

. . .

An Angel

an angel appeared
to three different men

and he said to the first:
if i gave you a
handful of putty
what would you do?

i would make it into a vase
said the man

and what would you do?
he asked the second

i would make it into a bird
said the man

and what would you do?
he asked the third

i would make it holler
said the man

and the angel stood a moment
as though he were listening

now, he said to the first man
because you would make it into a vase
the lord will fill you
with living water

to the second he said: and because
you would make it into a bird
the lord will bring you to fly
through the heavens

and because you would make it holler,
he said to the third, look out:
he will make you holler

. . .

Problem in Design

what if you like to draw
big flowers

but what if some sage has told
you that there is
nothing more
beautiful

nothing more
beautiful

nothing more
beautiful

than a
straight
line

what should
you draw:
big
flow
ers
?
straight
lines
?

i think
you should
draw

big
flow
ers

big
flow
ers

big
flow
ers

big
flow
ers

big
flow
ers

big
flow
ers

big
flow
ers

big
flow
ers

un
til

they

be

co

me

a

str

ai

gh

t

l

i

n

e

. . .

The Short Man

a short man who lived
in a low country

once said to
himself:

if i were to move
to the mountains
i might be happier

or again, if close
to the sea, it might
be better;

as it is
i see nothing
but towering
windmills

men who are
taller than i

& even children
who have grown
beyond me

the next day
he moved to the
mountains

what a beautiful
view, he said,
of the tiny houses
in that low valley;

the goats no bigger
than puppies: the
men little bigger than
dolls

he was quite
content

the north wind
rattled his house
but he stayed inside

an avalanche slid
right past it: he took
no notice;

in spring he walked
out again to watch the
flowers breaking open
in the valley

i like it in the
mountains, he said
to himself

and perhaps would
like it by the
sea

but to be a short
man & live in
a low country

is not, and perhaps
would never have
been

a satisfactory
role for me

. . .

Old Magician

a very old, very sick
magician once said to
his assistant: awk.

what's that? said the
assistant.

awk, said the magician,
by which i mean, for
god's sake listen to
my last commands.

o.k., said the assis-
tant: shoot.

mix one newt's egg.

yep.

with one toad's eye.

yeah.

with 15 measures of
cinnabar;

say the alexandrine
incantation

& put it under a cold
stone to cool.

that all? said the
assistant. no goat's
blood?

no goat's blood.

no scream from old
lady?

no scream from old
lady, said the magi-
cian.

how long do you want
it to cool?

4 days, said the magi-
cian.

& then?

then pour it into a
hole in the ground.

what's supposed to
happen then?

i'll tell you then,
said the magician.

the assistant did just about
as he was told:
in fact, by the time he had
disobeyed, obeyed,
& disobeyed again,
he had gotten
the whole thing right:
ingredients mixed,
incantation spoken,
solution cooled
& poured into the ground.

all right, said the
assistant, now what
do we expect?

nothing, said
the magician.
expect nothing.

nothing? said
the assistant.

then what did we
do the experiment
for?

all my life, said
the magician,
i've wanted to do
an experiment
that hoped for nothing
& accomplished nothing.

and now? said the
assistant.

i think i've done
it, said the magi-
cian. go out in the
garden & look.

the assistant went
out & was back in a
minute.

master, he said, in
the place in the garden
where i dug the hole
a tree is growing:
a golden tree

it has golden fruit
the color of newt's eggs

golden leaves, the
color of toad's eyes

a living trunk, the
color of cinnabar

& sings, it sings
like a tree full of
birds.

. . .

Therapist

a man came to me with the
following problem:

"my mother-in-law," he said, "despises me;
my creditors, once friendly, are now all over
me; my wife threatens to leave me tomorrow
unless i put the children in a better school;
my employers criticize the tone of my work
for what they call a failure of nerve. what do
you suggest i do?"

i turned a somersault for him & he felt
better.

. . .

Old Fable

some women were raking in a field
when one of them struck upon something
hard

digging it up they discovered it
to be a coffin

containing the body of a young man

who sat up and reviled them
for the vanities of the earth

they nailed the lid
back on the coffin

put it into the ground

and went on raking

. . .

The Circus of
the Sun

I was set up from eternity,
And of old,
Before the earth was made:

The depths were not as yet
And I was already conceived;
Neither had the fountains of waters
As yet sprung out;

The mountains with their huge bulk
Had not yet been established;
Before the hills
I was brought forth:

He had not yet made the earth
Nor the rivers,
Nor the poles of the world:
When he prepared the heavens,
I was there.

           —PROVERBS 8:22–27

. . .

Sometimes we go on a search
and do not know what we are looking for,
until we come again to the beginning . . .

. . .

morning

In the beginning (in the beginning of time to say
the least) there were the compasses: whirling in
void their feet traced out beginnings and endings,
beginning and end in a single line. Wisdom danced
also in circles for these were her kingdom: the sun
spun, worlds whirled, the seasons came round, and
all things went their rounds: but in the beginning,
beginning and end were in one.

And in the beginning was love. Love made a sphere:
all things grew within it; the sphere then encompassed
beginnings and endings, beginning and end. Love
had a compass whose whirling dance traced out a
sphere of love in the void: in the center thereof
rose a fountain.

. . .

Fields were set
for the circus,
stars for shows
before ever
elephant lumbered
or tent rose.

. . .

The Morning Stars

Have you seen my circus?
Have you known such a thing?

Did you get up in the early morning and see the wagons pull into
     town?
Did you see them occupy the field?
Were you there when it was set up?

Did you see the cook-house set up in dark by lantern-light?
Did you see them build the fire and sit around it smoking and
     talking quietly?

As the first rays of dawn came, did you see
Them roll in blankets and go to sleep?
A little sleep until time came to
Unroll the canvas, raise the tent,
Draw and carry water for the men and animals;
Were you there when the animals came forth,
The great lumbering elephants to drag the poles
And unroll the canvas?

Were you there when the morning moved over the grasses?
Were you there when the sun looked through dark bars of clouds
At the men who slept by the cook-house fire?
Did you see the cold morning wind nip at their blankets?
Did you see the morning star twinkle in the firmament?
Have you heard the voices of the men's low muttering,
Have you heard their laughter around the cook-house fire?
When the morning stars threw down their spears, and watered
     heaven . . .

Have you looked at spheres of dew on spears of grass?
Have you watched the light of a star through a world of dew?
Have you seen the morning move over the grasses?
And to each leaf the morning is present.

Were you there when we stretched out the line,
When we rolled out the sky,
When we set up the firmament?
Were you there when the morning stars
        Sang together
And all the sons of God shouted for joy?

. . .

Morning is quiet over the field. Clouds hang over it close
and full. The song of morning goes up from the grass;
the sun receives and returns it to clouds, bending over the
morning field, full of the song of the grass.

In a green straw Mexican hat, very gentle and shy,
Tina watches the morning. Belmonte's child. Her hair
is brown and shining, straight. She loves to go out into
her province. Air is summer blue, full of life,
eager to carry light and color.

This is the day when the people come walking slowly
to the outskirts of town; when over the field they come to walk
in the grass where the stakes are driven: rust and dew.
They stand in the morning field, watching.

"See him drag that chain. Look how he pulls it!"
At work in loose pajamas, elephants twist their trunks around
the tent poles lifting lightly, their faces and hides are
finely lined, maps of a land of mountains and rivers: they move
about in the tall grass,
lifting their great scalloped feet.

The men are on hand as witnesses;
"Look at the camel."
"Moulting, I guess."
"There must be something wrong with it."
Inwardly she weeps.

The big stuffed mat the leapers land on sits on the field.
The weary lie on it like Romans; or sit on it upright,
pensively on edge,
the little big-headed Bagonghi.
Thinking about his teeth. "I go downtown to see the dentist,
every day, every day."
Every day a different town.

The festivity of plumes on timothy grass,
water-filled young shoots up from the early ground aspiring
up in the early morning playing, they are wet with water of
sky, sprinkled by clouds, standing,

overshoulder peering at light on the field;
dart of birds, and look here: walkers walking in sky water;
drops on grass, hanging colors: light of sun in many colors,
all the colors, and the drop stands on the timothy grass
wondering will I fall to earth or will I rise to heaven?

Up every day for the festival,
today is the festival of walkers, walking:
Out of all the round year today, the day of its coming.
We the innocent grasses stand on tiptoes overshouldering
each other, looking toward the circle's center,
middle of the field where they stretch the skyworks.
Birds dart over us, pulling shadows through us.

. . .

Quietly the field waited;
She would be blessed with the wonder of creation.
Workers are arrived from another world; like visiting angels,
they speak their own language and put their questioners
off with jokes: rough trousers, blue denim shirts, flesh red
from the elements:
Their eyes look far back, and infinitely on. They penetrate
and do not appraise:
beholding all things before them with the innocence of light.
Strange visitors, when they meet
they fall to laughter,
their glances flash together like water in sunlight.

These are the ones who tug at the ropes and put up the tents;
roustabouts with chants and hammers, who drive the stakes that
hold in place the billowing firmament.

Bagonghi says, "I'll take your suitcase until Mogador
wakes up."

Stubby, bow-legged, he rocks from side to side, a tug in a
swell, as he crosses the field,
holding the bag an inch above the ground.
He opens the wide door of the trailer, stands on tip-toes,
swings the suitcase into the dark. "It'll be all right till
Mogador wakes up."
He comes back leaving the door ajar.

The ground of the field is rich and growing, but who
will eat the grass? Horses, camels, zebras.

. . .

A song rises up from the ground, herbs from the field.
Who will watch the green grass growing; who will hear
the song of earth?

Children who come to see the tent set up in the morning.

Three masts stand on a sea of canvas. Rope line loops
from one to another, drops in a gentle arc to the ground.
Bagonghi swings his hand toward the gesture in mid-air.

"Look! The big top!"

Who stretches forth the canopy of morning?

(Knowing the wonder to be born of her, hoping to bring forth
a son, a tree, in whose laughing and delicate shade the
children of innocence could rejoice, the field waited.)

. . .

We have seen all the days of creation in one day: this is
the day of the waking dawn and all over the field the
people are moving, they are coming to praise the Lord:
and it is now the first day of creation. We were there on
that day and we heard Him say: Let there be light. And
we heard Him say: Let the firmament be; and water, and
dry land, herbs, creeping things, cattle and men. We were
there in the beginning for we were there in the morning
and we saw the rising of the tent and we have known how
it was in the beginning. We have known the creation of
the firmament: and of the water, and of the dry land, and
of the creatures that moved in the deep, and of the crea-
tures that moved on the land, and of the creation of men:
the waking of acrobats. We have known these things from
the beginning of the morning, for we woke early. We rose
and came to the field.

. . .

They lie in slumber late, the acrobats;
They sleep and do not know the sun is up.
Nor does the Lord wake them,
Nor do the sun's rays touch them.
And the Lord, who has chosen them,
The Lord, who created them,
Leaves them in slumber until it is time.
Slowly, slowly, His hand is upon the morning's lyre,
Makes a music in their sleeping.
And they turn, and turning wonder
Eyes awake to light of morning.
They rise, dismounting from their beds,
They rise and hear the light airs playing
Songs of praise unto the Lord.
The circus is a song of praise,
A song of praise unto the Lord.
The acrobats, His chosen people,
Rejoice forever in His love.

. . .

Mogador comes down the field.

"There he is!"

He walks the earth like a turning ball: knowing
and rejoicing in his sense of balance:
he delights in the fulcrums
and levers, teeter-boards, trampolines, high-wires,
swings, the nets, ropes and ring-curbs of the natural
universe.

Beneath his feet the world is buoyant,
thin and alive as a bounding rope.
He stands on it poised,
a gyroscope on the rim of a glass,
sustained by the whirling of an inner wheel.

He steps through the drum of light and air, his
hand held forth.
The moment is a sphere moving with Mogador.

. . .

afternoon

Acrobat's Song

Who is it for whom we now perform,
Cavorting on wire:
For whom does the boy
Climbing the ladder
Balance and whirl—
For whom,
Seen or unseen
In a shield of light?

Seen or unseen
In a shield of light,
At the tent top
Where rays stream in
Watching the pin-wheel
Turns of the players
Dancing
In light:

Lady,
We are Thy acrobats;
Jugglers;
Tumblers;
Walking on wire,
Dancing on air,
Swinging on the high trapeze:
We are Thy children,
Flying in the air
Of that smile:
Rejoicing in light.

Lady,
We perform before Thee,
Walking a joyous discipline,
A thin thread of courage,
A slim high wire of dependence
Over abysses.

What do we know
Of the way of our walking?
Only this step,
This movement,
Gone as we name it.
Here
At the thin
Rim of the world
We turn for Our Lady,
Who holds us lightly:
We leave the wire,
Leave the line,
Vanish
Into light.

. . .

The tent is soaked in afternoon light. Filled with sound.
Pilgrims wander in at the wide door, full of wonder.
The expanse of it!

Waving walls.
Tiers of seats.
Can this have been built in one day?

They enter; parents guiding: they have seen more places.
Yet look: a child is leading.

Filled with wonder; the tent is strange; circus horses
    and circus men.
Clowns are from a far-off land.

The tent shuts out the wind, and heat, the dust and rain, and locks
    light in.

Through the wide door: they roll like marbles; first a few,
    and later many.
Tent-flap leads to the field beyond: performers cross; their plumed
    hats shake; their red and gold capes billow in the wind.

. . .

The family
Running lightly into the ring,
Lead one horse with them
and leave two others standing in the track.
There is a flourish of trumpets.
The Cristianis approach the center of the ring,
Raise their hands,
Smile,
and bow.
The music starts again;

The horse trots rhythmically around the ring,
Five Cristianis stand in a row,
Marking time,
In rhythm with the hoof-beats.
At a signal from Lucio
They run across the ring
To meet the horse
When he comes around.
They fork-jump as he passes
And land all sitting on his back.

                              Applause.

The horse runs halfway around;
The riders relaxed
Lift their hands to show how easily it is done.
Then they leap off,
Belmonte first,
Corky,
Ortans,
Mogador
And Oscar
Once more raise their hands and smile.

Music again,
The horse starts around
And the boys,
Belmonte,
Mogador,

Oscar
Make jumps to his back,
Land standing with arms upraised.
Leaping separately
But riding together.

As they come around
Lucio,
In baggy pants,
Oversized jacket and battered hat,
Steps out in front of the horse.

The boys shout: "Hey! get out of the way!"
Lucio doesn't.
The boys jump down from the horse.
"Get out of the way. What are you? Drunk?"
Lucio shrugs,
Walks over to the ring,
Sits down, and begins to ponder.

Again music.

The boys begin their run to the horse
When Lucio slides across the ring
Somersaults through the horse's legs
Over the ring-curb
Onto the track.

                                        Gasp.

He tries again from outside the ring.
Somersaults through the flying hooves
Into the ring.

Picking up a bamboo pole
He vaults magnificently
To the horse's back.
Trembling he lands
Standing on one foot
Flailing his arms,
Sure to topple.

Shouts.

At last he finds it:
The point of balance
Secure,
Both feet planted firmly,
He leans back
Thumbs in his pockets:
Never a doubt in his mind.

He pulls a newspaper from his hip pocket,
Slaps it open, begins to read,
Then turning
Still reading
He takes a huge step
Off the horse's tail
Like an old man
Descending from a bus.

. . .

Penelope and Mogador

One time Penelope the tightrope-walker asked Mogador
how he was able to land so gracefully after he did a
somersault on horse-back.
Mogador said:
>It is like a wind that surrounds me
>Or a dark cloud,
>And I am in it,
>And it belongs to me
>and it gives me the power
>to do these things.

And Penelope said, Oh, so that is it.
And Mogador said, I believe so.
The next day in the ring, Mogador leaped up on the horse.
He sat on it sideways and jogged half-way around the ring;
Then he stood up on the horse's back with a single leap;
He rode around balancing lightly in time to the music;
He did a split-jump—touching his toes with his hands;
He did a couple of entrechats—braiding his legs in
mid-air like a dancer:
Then Oscar threw him a hoop.
Mogador tossed it up in the air and spun it.
He caught it,
Leapt up,
And did a somersault through it!
He thought:
>I am a flame,
>A dark cloud,
>A bird;
>I will land like spring rain
>on a mountain lake
>For the delight of Penelope
>the tightrope-walker;

He landed on one foot, lost his balance, waved his arms
wildly, and fell off the horse.

He looked at Penelope,
Leapt up again,
Did a quick entrechat,
And Oscar tossed him the hoop.
He spun it into the air and caught it.
He did a somersault through it
And he thought:

> It is like a dark cloud, and I am in it;
> It belongs to me,
> And it gives me the power
> To do these things.

He landed on one foot, lost his balance, waved his arms
wildly and fell off the horse.
Penelope the tightrope-walker looked very calm.
Mogador leapt on the horse again.
Oscar frowned and tossed him the hoop.
He threw it into the air and caught it;
Leapt up and did a somersault through it.
He thought:

> I am a bird and will land like a bird!

He landed on one foot, lost his balance, waved his arms wildly
and fell off the horse.

> Now in the Cristiani family, when you fall off three times,
> They grab you by one ear,
> And bend you over,
> And one of the brothers
> Kicks you.

And that is what they did to Mogador.
Then the circus band started playing again.
And Mogador looked at Penelope:
Then he looked at the horse and flicked his ear with his hand;
He jumped up on the horse and landed smartly;
He stood up in one leap and caught the hoop;
He twirled it in the air and caught it again;
And then he did a somersault through it.
He didn't think anything.
He just did a somersault—
And landed with two feet on the horse's back.

Then he rode half-way around the ring
And got off with a beautiful scissors leap.
Penelope applauded,
And clasping her hands overhead, shook them
    like a boxer.
Mogador looked at her,
    then back at the horse,
And with a gesture of two arms he said
It was nothing.

. . .

Ortans

Ortans stands on one end of a teeter-board:
Mogador and Belmonte,
From the height of two tables
Jump
Down
And
Land
On the other end.

Ortans flips into the air,
Does a two and a half turn
And lands neatly in a high chair.
Relaxed as a rag doll,
Gracious as a queen,
Looking as though she had been there all afternoon.
She lolls a moment in the chair,
Gives the audience a glance
And a beautiful smile.

Then she daintily dismounts
Into her brothers' arms;
Lifts her right hand,
Curtseys on tiptoes and disappears.

. . .

La Louisa

Her toes almost touch the top of the tent;
She lies out, balanced at the arch of her back,
Her toes are pointed,
Her long slim legs stretch before her,
Her waist is taut,
Her whole body is semi-relaxed.

Her arms lie out gracefully behind her head,
Her long hair rides behind her as she swings forward:
There is a flower in her hair,
It hugs her head as she swings back.
Back and forth,
Back and forth.

Now she drops.
Head first:
Her hair
And the flower
Tumbling toward the ground.
Look away!

Precipito-
volissimo-
volmente!

She has caught herself,
Is hanging by her feet;
She swings back and forth,
Her back beautifully arched,
Her hands and fingers poised,
The flower riding in her long hair.

She pulls herself up,
Hangs by her hands,
Grasps the rope between her legs,
Slides down it to the ground.

Bows graciously,
Accepts applause
with lifted arm.

And leaves the ring.
. . .

Our dreams have tamed the lions,
have made pathways in the jungle,
peaceful lakes; they have built new
Edens ever-sweet and ever-changing
By day from town to town we carry
Eden in our tents and bring its won-
ders to the children who have lost
their dream of home.

. . .

evening

They are with me now, the golden people; their limbs
are intertwined in golden light, moving in a heavy sea
of memory: they come, the beautiful ones, with evening
smiles: heavy-lidded people, dark of hair and gentle
of aspect, whose eyes are portals to a land of dusk.
Their melancholy holds me now: sadness of princes, and
the sons of princes: the melancholy gaze of those I
have not seen since childhood.

For childhood was full of wonder, full of visions: the
boy on horseback, either in a dream or on the plain,
approaching: the two gypsy girls who stood together and
asked the mysterious question. Truth and the dream so
mingled in their eyes I could not tell which of the two
had spoken.

Once more now they are with me, golden ones,
living their dream in long afternoons of sunlight;
riding their caravans in the wakeful nights.

. . .

After supper light on fields, prairie, long yellow
light on fields aspiring, fields looking up grass singing
high grass singing yellow light on green grass growing,
the wide round horizon, the long tired light on the field
and the green grass high yearning up aspiring to heaven
to the dome sky heaven the grass growing up to the sky
and the light dying, the sun wearily sleepily smiling
lying down, with a sighing song, a long smiling sigh
over the fields and the grass rising, thin prayer rising
tufted to the air above the field to the sky the dome
sky thin made of light air the dome above the field and
the field breathing the air full rich golden grass smelling
sweet and tired with sun dying sun lying down, dying down
in west.

. . .

The sunset city trembled with fire, the air trembled
in fiery light, a fiery clarity stretched west across the
walks, the tongues of air licked up the building sides, the
wings of fire hovered over the churches and houses, steeples
and stores of the wide flat city that stretched to the sea.
The walk like a drum was stretched as though over the
hollow kettle of ground, the hollow darkness under the walk
resounded as he walked toward the sunset, and the street
glowed like a drum in firelight, like a drumskin glowed the
walk and road as he walked toward the light, walked slowly
toward the light through the fiery clarity of the burning
air now cooled with evening as sun set. Walls of glass
reflected the fire of sun, took fire from it, were kindled
and blazed bright, so as he walked down the drumskin city,
he was walled in fire and walked toward fire, and in the
fire dark caverns were, dark doorways in the walls of fire,
portals in the panes of brass where these men sat on folding
camp chairs waiting while the world went round, bald men
sat on folding camp chairs waiting while the world went
round, their drumskin heads took fire from the sun, kindled
and blazed, were copper drums, brass helmets glowing above
the drumskin walks, each in his dark portal surrounded,
tipped on his campstool in door's darkness; brass accent
in the walls of glass. In the fiery city they sat on
campstools waiting while the world went round.

This is our camp, our moving city; each day we
set the show up: jugglers calm amid currents, riding
the world, joggled but slightly as in a howdah, on
the grey wrinkled earth we ride as on elephant's
head.

. . .

The Dust of the Earth

The dust of the day hangs in the air,
Motes in the light,
Dust of the trampling multitude,
Dust of the elephants padding by,
Dust no one stirred till the circus came,
It hangs like a veil!
Dust of the earth
Riding the twilight,
Silently moving
Each sphere
Each molecule
Riding the air,
In wakening twilight
Could
Whirling
Turn to earth
To planets,
Support the verdure of creation
The moving animals and men,
Could raise from its own green growing
White clouds and dark
Alive with lightning,
Could ripple with seas
Flow with rivers
Reflect the waters,
The mountains and sky.

But where does the first mote come from?
The first gliding sphere?

. . .

the midway

The paintings on the sideshow walls,
The banners and signs
Are dark and strange:
"Look at the two-headed boy, the armless wonder,
The lion-tamer,
The harlem band,
The seal boy,
The sword swallower,
Fire-eater,
Tattooed woman,
Snake charmer
And the man who throws knives at his wife."

In the darkening twilight,
The last of sunset.
Banners
Heraldic and strange:
Beowulf lives here,
Ogres inside,
But gay, strange music,
Come in and look,
Stand considering on the midway
Soon you will come in and look.

. . .

Snake Charmer

"You see this snake?
He looks terrible, don't he?
But in the southwest where I come from
We got 'em like cats to kill mice."
She strokes his head,
Folds him gently,
And puts him back in the box.

Picking out a larger one,
She holds it aloft in both arms:
"This here is the same kind of snake,"
She says,
"Only bigger."

. . .

Dog Act

Girl in white ten-gallon hat, jewelled band;
white shirt jewelled sleeves;
white gauntlets jewelled with flowers and stars;
skirt, white doe-skin, fringed;
spurred and jewelled high-heeled boots,
white with red interior,
striding in a wash of small white dogs.

Yapping, prancing, barrel-walking,
ladder-climbing, table-mounting,
somersaulting
hopping at her hissed command
through tiny shiny hoops.

. . .

Colonel Angus

"I don't remember where he lived out there," said the
Colonel.
"I think it was . . . aaaah! that lion!"

It was time for him to go on;
The lion knew it and roared.

The Colonel went into the small cage carrying a folding
chair and a whip.
The lion, big and dusty, snarled and pawed at him,

Then he roared,
Angus snapped the whip,
The lion crouched and pounced.
Apparently alarmed,
The trainer dropped his chair,
Scurried from the cage,
Slipped through the steel door and sprung it behind him.
The audience was impressed.
The lion, furious, was left standing with his paws against the door.

"I think it was Pasadena!" said the Colonel coming lightly
down the steps.

. . .

night

Acrobat about to Enter

Star of the bareback riding act,
Dressed in a dark-red high-collared cape,
Black-browed,
Waiting with the others
To go in:

To enter
The bright yellow
Glare of the tent,

He stood on an island,
Self-absorbed.

At twenty-one
There was trouble in his universe.

Stars were falling;
Planets made their rounds
With grating axles:

The crown of stars in blackness
Was awry.

Clouds were rising,
Thunder rumbled;
He was alone,
Nobly troubled
Waiting a moment.

He waited with challenge,
Young and in solitude,
Mourning inwardly,
Attentive to the black, fiery current

In his mind,
He would not be comforted.

Swift water,
Falling darkness:
He alone could hear it.

Hoarded the sound,
Pulled his cape around it:
Bitter and intense,
But it was his:

Youthful secret,
Black and smoldering,
Not of the crowd;

It was his private woe,
And being private,
Prized.

. . .

Now in telling the story
Of the Cristianis
Their early beginning
And long-ago birth
And their rising from earth
To brightness of sunlight,
We tell of creation
And glory,
Of rising,
And fall:
And again of the rising
Where we are all risen;
For each man redeemed
Is risen again.

The spinning of the sun,
The spinning of the world,
The spun sun's span
On the world in its spinning,
Are all in the story
From its beginning;
And when it is spun
There shall be no unspinning.

. . .

Mogador is running along with the horse.
His eyes are serious, full of thought.
His mouth is a little open as he runs and breathes.
He is smiling a little.
His lips are thin.

As he runs,
Bending the knees,
Dancing lightly beside the horse,
He is in step with the horse.

They both land lightly.
They spring both from the earth;
Their movement is through the air.
Their feet drop lightly to earth
And push off from it.

And as they rise and fall,
Rise,
Fly,
And (momentarily) fall,
Their heads rise too
And fall in regular rhythm.

They rise
And the hair of the horse's mane clings to him,
Pointing to earth.

They drop down
And each hair of the white long mane
Remains in air.

The boy's hair too,
Dark silk
Rides close as he rises;
Then rises in the air
Falling lightly over his forehead
As he drops to earth.

They come around the ring.
The boy runs on the inside.
The horse trots along close to the curb.

The boy with his horse as they turn
in the ring are boy and horse running in
blue and green field: his hand is on the
horse's back the horse is to him as close as hand.

They round the turn, the boy is out of sight.
But now, behold!
He flies above the horse, holding a strap at his shoulders.
His feet fly out behind.
His toes are together and pointed like closed scissors.
Now he splits,
Sits riding bareback
Pointing his toes to the ground
Spinning beneath them.
His arms are held in air relaxed.

He rides lightly,
Barely touching,
His arms in air.
Then he leaps up
And with a pirouette begins his dance.
What was begun
As a run
through the field
is turned
to ritual.

. . .

Rastelli

Now the story of Rastelli is one they love to tell
Around the circus
He is a hero
Not because his work was dangerous
But because he was excellent at it
And because he was excellent as a friend.

He was good at juggling
At talking
At coffee

Loving everyone
He died juggling
For everyone

He died
Oscar said in a low secret voice
when he was 33

The age of our Lord

They loved Rastelli
And he loved them
Their loves flamed together
A high blaze

Ascending to the Sun of being

Rastelli was a juggler and a kind of sun
His clubs and flames and hoops
Moved around him like planets
Obeyed and waited his command
He moved all things according to their natures:
They were ready when he found them
But he moved them according to their love.

As dancers harmonize, the rising falling planets
mirrored his movements.

Rising, falling, rotating, revolving they spun on
the axis of his desire.
Clubs were at rest, he woke them and sent them spinning;
From which again they flew, until flying and falling,
Spinning and standing a moment in mid-air,
They seemed to love to obey his command,
And even dance with the juggler.

Seeing the world was willing to dance,
Rastelli fell in love with creation,
Through the creation with the Creator,
And through the Creator again with creation,
And through the creation, the Lord.

He loved the world and things he juggled,
He loved the people he juggled for.
Clubs and hoops could answer his love:
Even more could people.

Lover and juggler
Bearer of light
He lived and died in the center ring
Dancing decorously
Moving all things according to their nature

And there, before the Lord, he dances still.

He is with us on the double somersault;
The three-high to the shoulders;
He is with us on the Arab pirouette and the principal
act on horseback.
And in the long nights,
Riding the trucks between towns, Rastelli is with us:
Companion,
Example,
Hero in the night of memory.

. . .

He stood outside the horse truck, waiting for Mogador to come back, and he began to whistle. Across the field the men had taken down the sides of the tent and were moving about in dim light under the top, picking up trunks, ropes and equipment and packing it away. He began to whistle a tune from the depths of his soul; he had never heard it before but he recognized it as a form of the song his soul had always been singing, a song he had been singing since the beginning of the world, a song of return. It was as though he stood in a dark corner of the universe and whistled softly, between his teeth, and the far stars were attentive, as though he whistled and waves far off could hear him, as though he had discovered a strain at least of the night song of the world.

· · ·

By day I have circled like the sun,
I have leapt like fire.

At night I am a wise-man
In his palanquin.

By day I am a juggler's torch
Whirling brightly.

. . .

Have you known such a thing?
That men and animals
Light and air,
Graceful acrobats,
And musicians
Could come together
In a single place,
Occupy a field by night
Set up their tents
In the early morning
Perform their wonders
In the afternoon
Wheel in the light
Of their lamps at night?

Have you seen the circus steal away?
Leaving the field of wonders darkened,
Leaving the air, where the tent stood, empty,
Silence and darkness where sight and sound were,
Living only in memory?

Have you seen the noon-day banners
Of this wedding?

. . .

Postscript

Mogador,

I still haven't gotten to say the thing I want to say about you and the whole family. It is that, to a greater degree than almost anyone I know, you are what you are. You are an acrobat in a family of acrobats. And you have arrived at that generation in the family which is most to be desired, the time of ripeness, the moment of fullest awareness of function and responsibility of producing beauty, songs of praise.

You wanted to call this poem "Unfolded Grace." You said that early in the morning when we were both too tired to talk more, and you pointed out that it meant a lot of things. Unfolded Grace: the acrobat in somersault unfolding, landing lightly on horseback; the family in its generations unfolding, and arriving at the same moment, those same moments of unfolding grace.

Why talk about the somersault, the leap and landing as such a great thing? It is great and small. It is a high achievement for a man and no achievement at all for god or angel. It is proud and humble. It represents graceful victory over so many obstacles; the most elegant solution of so many problems. And yet like the blossoming of the smallest flower or the highest palm, it is a very little thing, and very great.

Think, Mogador, of the freedom, in a world of bondage, a world expelled from Eden; the freedom of the priest, the artist, and the acrobat. In a world of men condemned to earn their bread by the sweat of their brows, the liberty of those who, like the lilies of the field, live by playing. For playing is like Wisdom before the face of the Lord. Their play is praise. Their praise is prayer. This play, like the ritual gestures of the priest, is characterized by grace; Heavenly grace unfolding, flowering and reflected in the physical grace of the player.

I had a friend, a Hindu monk named Bramachari, whose monastery near Calcutta was called Sri Angan, which he translated as "The Playground of the Lord." That is the key to the whole matter, the monks playing joyously and decorously before the Lord, praising the Lord. The playground, though sown with tares, is a reflection of Eden. I think there can be a "Circus of the Lord."

For we are all wanderers in the earth, and pilgrims. We have no

*permanent habitat here. The migration of people for foraging & exploit-
ing can become, with grace (in the latter days), a travelling circus. Our
tabernacle must in its nature be a temporary tabernacle.*

*We are wanderers in the earth, but only a few of us in each genera-
tion have discovered the life of charity, the living from day to day, receiv-
ing our gifts gratefully through grace, and rendering them, multiplied
through grace, to the giver. That is the meaning of your expansive, out-
ward arching gesture of the arm in the landing; the graceful rendering,
the gratitude and giving.*

. . .

One Island

I.

cir
cle

of
brown

cir
cle

of
blue

cir
cle

of
brown

cir
cle

of
blue

cir
cle

of
earth

cir
cle

of
earth

cir
cle

of
sea

cir
cle

of
sea

. . .

cir
cle

of
brown

cir
cle

of
brown

cir
cle

of
blue

cir
cle

of
blue

cir
cle

of
earth

cir
cle

of
earth

cir
cle

of
sea

. . .

com
ing

of
dark

com
ing

of
dark

com
ing

of
light

com
ing

of
light

com
ing

of
dark

com
ing

of
dark

com
ing

of
light

. . .

earth
cir
cle

earth
cir
cle

sea
cir
cle

sea
cir
cle

. . .

brown earth
brown earth

blue   earth
blue   earth

brown sea
brown

    sea

blue   sea
blue

. . .

pres
ence

of
light

pres
ence

of
light

pres
ence

of
dark

pres
ence

of
dark

pres
ence

of
dark

pres
ence

of
dark

pres
ence

of
light

. . .

dark   land
dark   land
light   sea
light   sea

dark   land
dark   land
light   sea
light

. . .

leaf   leaf
sound   sound

leaf   leaf
sound   sound

wave   wave
sound   sound

wave   wave
sound   sound

. . .

```
land              land
smell             smell

land              land
smell             smell


sea               sea
smell             smell

sea               sea
smell             smell
```

. . .

com
ing

of
dark

com
ing

of
dark

com
ing

of
light

com
ing

of
light

   com
   ing

   of
   dark

   com
   ing

   of
   dark

   com
   ing

   of
   light

. . .

II.

black   red
rocks   earth

black   red
rocks   earth

green   red
leaves   earth

green   red
leaves   earth

black   black
rocks   rocks

black   black
rocks   rocks

green   green
leaves   leaves

. . .

light   light

cuts   cuts

shad   shad
ow   ow

shad   shad
ow   ow

cuts   cuts

light   light

                . . .

stone   leaf
shad   shad
ow   ow

stone   leaf
shad   shad
ow   ow

leaf   stone
shad   shad
ow   ow

leaf   stone
shad   shad
ow   ow

. . .

land
wind

land
wind

sea
wind

sea
wind

sea
wind

sea
wind

land
wind

land
wind
. . .

hill   hill
shad   shad
ow   ow

hill   hill
shad   shad
ow   ow

cloud   cloud
shad   shad
ow   ow

cloud   cloud
shad   shad
ow   ow

. . .

```
land            sea
cir             cir
cle             cle

land            sea
cir             cir
cle             cle


sea             land
cir             cir
cle             cle

sea             land
cir             cir
cle             cle

        . . .
```

leaf   leaf
sound   sound

leaf   leaf
sound   sound

wave   wave
sound   sound

wave   wave
sound   sound

. . .

goat's goat's
cry cry

goat's goat's
cry cry

bird's bird's
cry cry

bird's bird's
cry cry

. . .

is
land

is
land

one
is
land

one
is
land

is
land

one
is
land

one
rock

one
sea

. . .

Port City:

The Marseille Diaries

travelling miles
by train
and bus
and foot

waiting for trains at night
on empty platforms

walking alone
down monsieur-le-prince
with dawn coming

running to catch the
last train out of
paris

the sound of the river
the whisper of the river
below the bridge

the lights
in the river

light is blue
and grey
the color
of life

the mist
the slight cold
the presence of water

the vastness
of the sky
and the
comparative
loneliness

(to be in
a throng of
strangers
is still
to be alone)

strange music
in the ancient
fairgrounds

the eyes
of strangers

the moments passed
like parables

the joy
of being
alone
and in
a foreign
land

. . .

lights in the water

the mogador
clam vendor

the upstairs
lobster house

georges' indignation
at the prices

seaweed
and lemons

the lobster houses
off the narrow street

little restaurants
small cafes

affiches for
(bullfights)
in seville
or nîmes

the hedges
lights reflected
in the rain
on hedges

gangster palaces
cafe maritime

bouillabaisse houses
tablecloths for tourists

shoemaker with
the aluminum leg

turkish shoemaker
in the phonebooth
shop

the high old wall of
buildings along the
quayside

the steep approach to
n-d de la garde

glass atop
the stone walls of
baumettes

witches at the
other end of town

the potter's field
and theo's
grave

georges' friend
(was his name
ferdi?)

la ste baume
ste marie magdalen
(madelaine)

l'abbaye de st victor
et st lazare

café
arrosé
à rhum

la nuit
des arabes

rue robert

le petit
accordionist

le volga

rue
des assassins

luigi
runs for
the wine

georges borrows
glasses

one knife
one loaf of bread
one can of sardines
for five

and sometimes chocolate:
a single bar divided

la tosca
(the lady was
a fence)

the monkey
in the basket
in the cafe
in the alley

nightclerk
agile, small-boned
smiling
chic

places for coffee
along the boulevard

le gâre st charles

its terrace with the view

and then the
long descent to the
street

marseille

marseille

. . .

i will sing you
of the moments
sing you
of those
possibly
meaningless moments

(rain on tendril,
drops of rain
on a tendril)

(i will sing you
somewhat of those
moments)

the times
the moments
at pescara

the sun on the field
the bright white sun
on the sand of the field

the tent
in the afternoon

the tent
on the crowded evening

(i will sing you
somewhat of pescara)
. . .

and the whisper of the waters in the bay
the darkness of the waters
the lights (the deep lights)
that rode on the waters

notre dame (in
lumination)
on the waters

the cool of the evening
in the window
the sound of the street
rising
and echoing in the water

the voices
of the arab
legionnaires

and all the time dolly
dolly is drawing
her picture

how to give you that picture:
the picture of those days

bear down; try hard
no, i will talk
in this manner:

in rumination
lived i the moment
and in rumination
sing it

i was not here
nor there
in those moments
but only sometimes
there:

yet all the time
in every moment

passing
was the song:

the song
was living
and the moments
joined the
song

the song was singing
as i walked (or
wandered)

the song was singing
as i went
(or strayed).

this was the song that was
singing every moment
the song my heart
was hearing
(as i strayed)

. . .

rain in that city
and sound of siren
hee haw
hee haw
hi lo
hi lo
through the
city

sitting in
the church
and hearing
hi lo
hi lo
(like a drunkard
reeling through
the town)

rain
and wind on the water
grey sky
(no clouds)

and cold
(a wind
goes through
you)

rain
the city overcast
with lead

wander at the far side
but keep an eye
on home

rain
(the girls of rain
across the steppes
of wave)

winds from
everywhere

the overcast day

the light behind
the sky

a sea wind
a wet wind
leaving the ropes
hang cold and wet

and moving the little boats
in the bay

a tugging wind

afternoon
in an ancient city
of wide stone plazas
and a quay

i know

i know
where i
am

i am on the far side of the bay
and my room is over there

my home is there

hôtel du calais

to take the
trolley
to a far place
or to go home

now
before the
storm

who would know?

i could ask
the shoemaker
with the aluminum
leg

(i could ask
the light behind
the sky)

the light behind
the sky:

go slowly
home

                . . .

freddy
lived at the
hôtel des
trois
something

while georges
stayed with me
at the calais

but freddy
was always
there
mending shirts
or boiling tea
or setting
the alarm
clock

georges
was the laundry
expert
every day
was laundry

savon
le chat

shirts
in the basin
lines stretched
through the room
everyone's
in a single
wash
georges'
ramon's
fernand's
luigi's
mine

raymond's
was never
(and never would be)
included

but yvonne
let him
sleep in
her bed
while she
and the other girl
from the bar
des états
washed
and ironed
and mended
his clothes

they used
to feed him
too,
at least
for a while

the man at the
post office
waiting
for his wife

three days
since she
had left
(walked out)
and he had
had no word
of her

the bearded
beggar
who danced
for a child

and told me
later he
was (or had
been) a
poet

one morning,
leaning on
a parapet,
he showed me
a passport
of the kempt
parisian young man
he had been

we would travel
together,
he said that same
morning,
he and i
to the
holy land

and theo
had dreamt
as well
of a voyage
to israel

yvonne
longed to be
a stewardess
on a paquebot
to jaffa

marcel
was back
and forth
from
casablanca

the brighteyed
spoon-faced
little old man
from the chamber
of commerce
who was a
friend of
monsieur
pierrot's

pierrot's
harried
and well past
middle-aged
sister

his two
little boys

his white-
haired jolly
father from
milan

with the dapper
bow tie

. . .

remembering
the city

remembering
the city

a million
disparate
moments
make the
whole

(whose city
was this city?
it was
mine)

mine,
because i
could only see
what i was
ready to see

mine

because i
had been coming
toward it
since

(before the
plague ship
first arrived
in port)

before st
lazarus
and mary
magdalene
first
came
ashore

before
ste sarah
greeted
them

before
the phoenicians
landed
on that
shore
to trade
with
gauls

i had
been coming
toward that
city
since
the beginning
of time

i had
been coming
toward
that city
and singing
that city's
song

. . .

across
the port
the garrison
light of
the bay
is blue
as silk

cool of
the evening
on the quay

the bar
des colonies
is lit

madame
is not
descended
yet in
rouge and spit-
curls
and her
flowered
dress

(dolly
sits at
the table
now
drawing
the picture
of a flower)

look
at this,
says dolly;
i'm an
artist

krevkor
and his
friend
are having
an aperitif

la tante
is working
the bar

buy me a
drink, says
dolly, eh?

not him,
says the aunt,
he hasn't got
money for
no drink

i'll give
you a piece
of candy,
says krevkor's
friend

in the long
summer evening
the dusk
comes late,
but comes at last
to the long
stone quay

and lights
go on
in the rooms
upstairs
the rooms
with closed shutters

the rooms
with open shutters
the rooms
with four socks
hanging
in the window

. . .

oh dolly
was fat
she was
fat fat fat
and she wore
a low-cut
tightfitting
black
dress

her eyebrows
were painted
her lashes
were beaded
her mouth,
a perfect bow

her mind
was a child's:
a sweet, hope-
ful child's

she was always
drawing
her picture

giselle
was cross-eyed
and wore huge
pearl earrings
and three
strands of pearls
around her
stubby neck;
she was sweet, too;
but not so hopeful;
she knew how it would be
and it always was

the aunt:
the aunt

is another
story:
the aunt
had come out
of the sea

the mailman
a perfect mailman
his face
was part
of his
uniform:
particularly
the moustache

dolly
was drawing
her picture
and she
showed it
to the mailman:
look, monsieur louis,
i'm an artist

oui, he said,
vous êtes une
grande artiste

hopefully
dolly looked
to the others:
look, she said,
i'm an artist

. . .

the bar
des colonies
is full of
mirrors

back of the bar
and on the back wall
and again
around at the side

the port
is reflected
in the mirrors:
the port
and the street
and the passers-
by

at night
madame
comes down
in her flowered
dress
with rouge
on her cheeks
and on her lips
her hair
pulled tight
in a bun
at the side
and spitcurls
in front
of each ear

beaded
earrings
hang and
shake;
a necklace
and a quiet
bracelet

at night
her heels
are high
and hard
to walk in

but at night
she mostly
sits
and talks
to the girls

or to a
senegalese
soldier
or to a
couple of
german foreign
legionnaires

madame stays
downstairs
till eleven
or twelve;
after that
you must
pound on
the hotel
door
to wake
her up
to let
you in

she buzzes
to release
the lock
and then
as you get
to the first floor
she appears

behind the glass door
of her apartment
in a negligee
to ask:
"qui est-ce?"

(the only
possible
answer is:
c'est moi)

il faut
then
that she gives
you the key
(a huge one
that hangs
from a great
metal star)
she opens
the door
a crack
and hands
it out:

bonsoir!

bonsoir

you continue

to climb
to number five:

your room

across the hall
from krevkor's

. . .

on summer nights
krevkor
slept
with his
door open:

a child
in a crib

he tossed
from side
to side

on summer
evenings
he would
stand
shirtless,
leaning
on his elbows
looking out
across
the bay

waiting
to go
to America

waiting
for permission

till the
quota
would let him
in

his name
was on
the list

a few months
more

another
year

when he went
he would
take the
plane

he had
a picture
of the plane:

a golden nose
four motors
on a blue
postcard

he would live
with his aunt
and uncle
in ohio

but until then
he would wait

his friend
advised the boat:
a transatlantic
steamer

every night
after dinner
they would talk
about the boat
and plane,
calmly at first
but then
excitedly

near the window
and the view
a little table

and near the table
a small
two-burner
stove

krevkor
cooked on
the stove
ate at
the table
washed in the basin
and kept his clothes
in the closet
(which stood
against the wall
between the beds)

he shaved
in the mirror
and when
he went out
for the evening
dressed
he looked
immaculate

somewhere
on his floor
there was
a shower
(but i never
found out
where)
somewhere
in a dark hole
boxed in wood
there was a
shower
krevkor
used

krevkor
in the white shirt
the night he had
gone visiting
on sunday

stop by in my room,
i had said,
when you return

and at ten or
ten thirty
he knocked on the door

wearing the white shirt
a jacket
and perhaps
a red tie

his hair was back
in a polish pompadour

it always was
but this time
it had been worked on

he stood beneath
the naked bulb
and loosened his tie
and we talked
about philosophy

the philosophy
of lending

the philosophy
of giving

such a one
i would help

and such a one
i would not

if such a one
wanted two thousand francs
i would lend it to him
or i would not

i would give it to him,
yes: but i would not lend;
i would not expect it back

if i gave it to him
i would not expect him
to repay

(i thank you
for that

i thank you
for saying that

i feel
that if you are here
and behaving thus

it is as though
i were here

you do my work
while i
am away

you are my
vicar
here)

in this town
what i give
i do not expect
to see again

and what i cannot give
i cannot lend

. . .

the city has been there
waiting
(and not waiting)
for the moment

the city is
your family's
far-off
home

the city knows you

yet is asleep
but will return
your smile

the city knows you

you have first
caught sight of her
at this moment
from the hill

from the hill now
you descend
into the city

light
(of the sun)
in a curve
of the wave

mist
(mere gas
fumes)
rising

the stone quay
and the sound
of the waters

nets stretched
from the mast
to the bow

the silverbellied
fish
on racks
and
in baskets

the blackhaired
fisherwoman
and her pale son

wrinkled forehead
and flashing smile

the greyhaired fisherwoman
and her daughter

in the middle
of the afternoon

i stand between
the port
and la canebière

and behold the city
as though it were

a dream
or memory

i try
to hold the city

i try to breathe it in
(i breathe it into my lungs
and i embrace it)

city, city
loved by me
because known by me;
known because loved:
i love thee

i embrace thee

city, city
i am in thy midst
as a dream in thy midst
and thyself
as a dream
in me

(city, city,
i am in thy midst,
as a dream in thy midst;
and myself
in the midst
of my dream)

city, city
i ask thee
not to change

i ask thee
not to stay;
but only to be,
and let me be
with thee

(i stand between
the water

and the city's
artery

and speak thus
to my familiar
city)
  . . .

Part II

still at the port
still at the port
sunset
strange blue over the water
legion garrison
in the distance
sun in west
looking out over
the ancient waters
knowing
where i am
understanding
where i am
here
at this window
looking out
over the water

buildings
on the other side
the old buildings

buildings
of a foreign land

i am here

here at last
here to enjoy
this moment
in this city

how old the waters are
what they have known
how old the stone
what it has known

lazarus
and mary magdalene
the plague ship
the italian architects

these buildings
were the scenes
of splendor

her heart was broken
waiting
in this city

i am here
am here at last
i have been coming
forever
to this city

no, it is not
the lady on the hill
who speaks

it is not
my heart

the water
speaks to me

and i
to the water

i speak
to the depth
of the water

and to the stone
beneath the water

i have been coming
forever
to this city

garrison
i know
that garrison

beacon
pharos

i know
that light

water
i know
these waters,
know
these waters

i know
this setting
of the sun
this moment

i have been coming
forever
to this city

(a fact
which makes
my adventures
so much the less
noteworthy)

and i have been singing
this city's song

water
sky
and stone:
movement
of weather
the drifting
of wind

timelessness:
not timelessness
but longer time
than this
my body
knows

the ancient
and enduring
sea

the ancient
and enduring
stone

not history
but meaning:
ancient meaning
in the ancient
stone:

the sun
the sea
the rock
beneath the sea:

we stand
as witness

we stand
as witness
to its turning
and to its stance
and flow:

i have come
forever
to this city
i know its water
know its stone
i know its ancient
light

speak to me:
it speaks to me,
and to its heart,
my heart

not this city
but this setting;
not this setting,
but this world

my heart
is at the city's
heart;
the water's
heart;
the heart
of stone;

and i have come
forever
to this city

. . .

the morning show

the afternoons

the evening

one town
at many
different
times
of day

at different
times of year

the same
strange town

(the same
short street
which stretched
from end to
end of that
short quay)

a single
string:

a single
taut-stretched
string

(there
where all the
music was
held tight
in that
one-fretted
instrument)

a single string
a single street

was stretched tight
by the waters

to walk
upon
those
stretched-
tight
strings
was
music

the street
in sun

the street
in rain

the early
morning
street

like a
budding
flower

the early
morning
street

like a
budding
rose

. . .

waiting, sitting
in the doorway
in the late
afternoon

with the evening
coming on

waiting
for theo
to come back

sitting
in the doorway
on a wooden stool
waiting for him
to return

he would
come with the wine
and the salade russe

but now
he was gone

the sky
was high

i leaned
against the door-frame
and was happy

this little hut
in this city:
familiar hut
in an oriental
city

an eternal
situation
a timeless
wooden stool

the sky
blue sky
pale sky
was high

(and full
of mysteries)

when he came back
we would light
the candle
and eat whatever
it was
and drink
the wine

we would talk
about the days
(his days)
in poland

or he would read me
a word at a time
from an english
grammar

or show me
his papers

sometimes
he would show me
his jack-knife
his watch
and tell me
where and how
he had gotten them

sometimes would
bring me
a small surprise
(a flashlight?
a nail?)

from out
of the other
room

when it came
time to go
(which was
always very early—
9:30 or 10)
he would walk me
through the little
cluttered yard

to the wooden door
which he padlocked
for the night;

we would shake hands then
and smile

and i would
walk home
down the long
rue roger salengro
past the arch
and through
the arab section
to the port

. . .

the wind tugged at the water
the rain tugged at the clouds

water slapped against the quays

oil rode upon the water
the grey sun rode the wave

raymond approached down the quay
a thing of terror

his shapeless felt hat
made him tall

his many coats
were hunched about
his shoulders

an ichabod man
a walking windmill
a satanesque
clochard

panhandling
panhandling
up and down
the quays

he terrified
his would-be
benefactors

as though
the day itself
had taken form
and now
was raymond

a great
rudder-nose

a great
(prognathous)
jaw

as sad
as the day
he wept
as now
the sky
as now
the sea

five francs
twenty francs
from bewildered
citizens
and frightened
strangers

he dropped them
into a formless
outer pocket

and when
there were
enough
would buy
white wine

le philosophe

his expression too
was philosophic

he lifted
a single eyebrow
and looked calmly
off to sea

his cheeks
were ruddy
and his face
was of the north

blue-eyed
a bright
blue eye
his beard
was white
and short;
his beret
at a smart
(but not
a rakish)
angle

on his left foot,
a worker's shoe,
and on his right
a backless bed-
room slipper

his coat
an army coat
was belted in
and billowed out
an inch
above his ankles

he stood
beneath a leaking swing
and looked beyond the fairground
toward the sea

(i tried
to take his picture
and he scowled)
and muttered
that police-informers
often ended
in the bay.

        . . .

states of being

with every state
of being
a different
view

a different
aspect
of the (changing)
city

the focussed
and unfocussed
states

the higher
the state
the higher
the vision

(let us set down
that a certain
flash of sunlight
on a certain
wave of water
struck my eye)

(that i noted
the antiquity
of elegant facades
along the waterfront)

that as long
as the city
is remembered
(by me)
the bend of the bay
and the face of the church
at sunset
(will be remembered)

at noon
along the cobbled
quay
the shadow
of a gull

if i were dead
and looked
back down
upon the city
(maudlin now)
if i were dead
and looked back down
upon the city
would i see
the city still
as i remember?

i would look
from a line
above the bay
a central point
a little south
of center
a line above
the wide stone walk
about the point
at which the great ships
dock

i would
look down
upon the city
to see if it
was my
(beloved) city

still

to see
if there was

still that movement;
still that movement,
still that peace.

in varying
states of being
a varying
city

the music of twilight
was a purple music
music of dusk and autumn
a sad parade

(the music of autumn
was bythnia: a mixture
of people; of berbers
and moslems moving
beneath the trees
before the storefronts)

(the man
on the hill
with the high
steel pole
who had taught
his monkey
to climb it)

(the man
on an even
higher hill
who beat a drum
slapped a tambourine
and shook bells
on his head
as he danced)

there is
a dancer
above the city

a dancer
above the city
who comprehends
the city's ways

. . .

georges
was a russian
and had been
a legionnaire;
the first time i saw him
was at the tosca,
i noticed him because
he looked
like a type
from a gangster movie:
not really the brains,
not really the lug,
but a trustworthy type
to strangle you
from the back

his face,
a slavic face,
was angular
and the light
came upon it
from the tile floor
of the little bar
at noon

the next day
when he wasn't there
i asked madame
the owner of the tosca
who he was,
was he her husband?
(i had thought he was)
but she said: oh, no—
he was just someone
who hung around there;
that was obvious.

the morning after that
i was walking by there again
and he darted out.

hello he said
(or maybe "hello, joe")
hello
ça va?

ça va, i said, et vous:
ça va?
non, he said, ça ne va pas.

why not?

oh, he said,
been out of work.

do you have a room
in the hotel?
georges asked,
and i said yes.
can i stay there with you?
don't you have any place to stay?
i haven't right now.
ok, i said
i'll come up tonight
all right, i said
i'll see you there
around nine o'clock

at a quarter of nine
georges was there

i wanted to talk to you
about a plan, he said.

and he told me all about
running the clocks
over the border from belgium

he told me he was russian
and that he had been
brought up in turkey

then the foreign legion

then the contrabanding

and now
hard times

he only wanted
a little money

25 dollars
(25,000 francs?)

to get started again

he would make a lot of money

he would set me up
(with my portable typewriter)
in a magnificent
waterfront apartment

war had made him
tired of war

there was only
one thing
worth seeking

not adventure,
no; not this
not that,
but peace.

with this
i heartily
agreed

there was
no bird like
peace

there was nothing
else worth
bending your thoughts
to
but that

(i had come
as a matter of fact
to marseille
with my alpenstock
to search
for peace
and to recruit
a tiny band
of men
to work
for peace)

for the moment
we had our plans
to make:

he to run the clocks
and i to avoid
making even the suggestion
that i could make
a loan
(for i could not)

i lay
on the high
wide bed,
my head
against the
long (cylindrical)
bolster

georges sat
backward on the
room's only chair
his arms crossed
on the back,
chin resting on them

his only
signs of pathos

were the holes
in his trousers
and in his shoes
and possibly
in the white
malnourishment
of his skin

shall i
turn out
the light?
he said
at last

no, get into
bed; i'll
turn it out

it was best
for him
to sleep
near the wall;
i'd be getting up
earlier
in the morning

. . .

there was a little
russian restaurant
(not the volga)
on a street
that led away
from the port

i had found it
by myself
one night
and had had a good
time there

a pretty waitress
came and sat
with me;
an old pot-bellied
russian drunk
sang songs
(at his own
invitation)
and the little
russian accordion-player,
drunk too,
made a lot of music

it must have been
the first time
i had seen him

now georges and i
went by one night
for borscht;
georges spoke
a little russian
to the waitress
and it began
to look
like a pretty good
evening

when the steamy
front door opened
and a couple
of red-faced cops
came in
and asked us
for our papers;

i had mine
but georges'
carte de séjour
had long expired

the gendarmes
used their
flashlight
on the date
and then took
georges along
with them
to the station.

he didn't
get back
that night
and i blamed
myself for having
thought
of the restaurant
(in fact,
for having
first gone there)

but the next
morning
(by the time
i got back
from church and coffee)
he was there.

it was nothing,
he said,
in fact,
they had extended
his papers

he would have
to get out
of the country
soon, but
at least,
not right
away

at noon
he suggested
we try the same place
again for a dish
of borscht
(he had figured
to the franc
what it would cost
for borscht and bread
and decided
it would be better
this once
than our usual
lunch in the room)

we ordered coffee
too (when lunch
was over) and
while we were
drinking it
two men
(one a man,
one hardly more
than a boy)
came up to the table

and said hello
to georges

georges greeted
them like old friends
asked them to sit down
at the table
and ordered
more coffee

the boy,
luigi,
was blond
and from milan;
the man was
fernand:
short dark
spanish;
he had a
moustache and
wore a beret;
the two
middle fingers
of his right hand
were missing

his french
was poor;
luigi's
even worse,
besides which
both were shy

it took me
quite a while
to realize
that meeting
them there
was no coincidence:

georges had first
met them
the night
before
in jail:
their papers
were even worse
than his

and he had told them
to meet him here
at noon

it took me a while
even after that
to realize
we had
adopted them
but this
we had

they were ours
both night and day:
the first night,
for example,
they were ours
as four in a bed

the next night
they had a room
and we had a room
and so it continued
for several nights,
perhaps for a week,
but was getting expensive

until at last
we heard
of the brothers
hospitallers

that was when
we began our
evening marches
up to their night-time shelter:
i with my crazy
alpenstock
and they with their
innocent miens

it cost about
40 francs,
which wasn't much

and in the morning
(it must have been
about 6 o'clock)
they'd arrive again
to sit around my room

(no word
can be itself
outside its context:
the bad words
and the good
all fall in place
as the wheel
goes round)

through the day
the window-ledge
(of the room)
was hot in the sun

ours was the only window
always open

fernand and luigi
would sit or lean on it
and look back
into the room:
i would too,

and look out
at the street

fernand would sometimes
use it as a bank
for his grenouille:
a little green
black speckled
wind-up frog
with a well-formed head
and pretty legs
who hopped along
in an eager
winning way

fernand
had brought it
with him
over the mountains
and through the snow
from spain

luigi liked it
and even georges
considered it
very clever

fernand
kept it
in his pocket
and brought it out
whenever he wanted
to think

the frog would hop
across the ledge
in the sun
and fernand would
watch it
with thought
behind his eyes

he used to
talk to me
about the days
in spain:
he joined
a monastery once
for a couple of months
but it hadn't worked;
and now he had left
to get away from franco

luigi
had left milan
to see the world
and to get away
from a life
of poverty
there

he hadn't thought
about papers
or anything else;
came over the border
at an unwatched point
and hitch-hiked from there
(as he had from milan)
to marseille

he met fernand
one day at the port
where both were looking
for a ship to work on;
and stayed with him
(probably in the street)
for a couple of days
until the night
they were rounded up
for papers

. . .

Part III

Part III

the letter
from brother octavius
said:

come and stay
as long as
you like

to rome

come and stay
with the trappists

the general house
on via santa prisca

but (merton's)
letter said:

be sure
to stop
at la
salette

i said
to the philosophe

i am going
to a monastery
up in the mountains

and spend a
month
(in medi-
tation)

he said:

that is good
(we all need
meditation)

i said
to georges:

i am going
i must go

i cannot stay
here any longer
(i am beginning
to fall apart)

he said:
you must not go

i said:
no: it is true:
i must

he said:
tell me only
in which direction
you are going:
north, south,
east, west

tell me
only the direction
and i will
find you

i said:
i believe you

he said:
tell me
the direction

i said:
east

and georges
said:

i will
find you.

. . .

the tale
is like
a spider's
web
spun out
and swallowed
in

the tale
the tale
a silver
thread
spun out
and swallowed
in

a single
match-stick
on the quay

a morsel
merest
morsel
of a
rind

(all at
the far
side
the far
side
of the
quay)

i walked
alone
one day
at noon
toward
the bridge

that led
to the
legion
garrison

toward
the little
inlet
(with
plekhanov's
boat)

the sun
stood on
one hand
above the
town

but straight
above the town
its light
fell straight
upon the
street
and every
ray
was like
a string
each living
ray
was like
a string
of music

each object
then leapt
from the street
and spoke:
each object

said its
name

proclaimed
its name
in glory
and its
being

and i
sang too:
my heart
sang too,
to know
each object
in its name
and being

to know
that all
indeed
was real

all had
history
and a
name

(as though
the moment
had been
rapt beyond
itself
and was eternal
while it
moved
in time)

i saw
each object
then in

its relation
(to a
timeless
being)

and my
heart
sang
(but kept
its deepest
peace)

and i
turned
and went
back
to the
boys
in the
room
. . .

A Greek Journal

Introduction

When I left New York for Greece I had hoped only to find a quiet place to live for a while and write some poems. Quiet and inexpensive. If I could have found an uninhabited island where I could forage for myself, I think I'd have gone there. I did not come looking for people, or for nature, much less for history: just for quiet. I thought I needed it for my work, as a photographer needs a darkroom.

Quiet? A place to get away from people? Bright light, loud noises, and a constant presence of people (and of birds, goats, fish) is more the style. You are never alone in Greece. Someone is always with you, right with you or watching from across the hill: watching, listening, never sleeping, gathering data for a fund that's been growing for the past several thousand years, watching for any flick of variation in patterns already known of human behavior. Wherever you live in Greece, whatever you do, wherever you sleep, you are doing it on a brightly lighted stage. Each day is judgment day.

I see this now. I hardly did when I first came to the islands in the early rainy months of 1964. The people who lived on the island were charming: they would not be overlooked. I tried to write about them as quickly as I could, to get over my first impressions, to get on with writing the poems I'd come to do.

this is the afternoon and so it is time to make a poem of the afternoon,
to come up from under it with a long sigh and to swing into it from
above: the afternoon, the golden time: to have no subject but the world,
life and the world, life in the world, the texture of life, the texture of
every minute as it passes

this is the afternoon and so it is time to make a poem of the afternoon
(the afternoon is making a poem of itself)

afternoon, the afternoon, the people stand on the sunlit quay and wait
for the kanaris

they stand on the quay and wait for the boat: the kanaris to arrive . . .

a long afternoon: an afternoon in the sun

the people stand in a kind of hushed silence; waiting for the boat to
appear on the (blue) horizon

an afternoon of hushed sunlight

a time of afternoon: the people stand in classical poses waiting for the
traditional return of the boat to the island

and wait for the boat to appear on the blue horizon

a golden afternoon: when sunlight like honey is poured on the land

they stand in hushed silence and nobody speaks

they are all there, all there, everyone from the town is there

they stand on the quay in the hush of waiting and look toward the
(blue) horizon

this is the afternoon, a time to make a poem (of the afternoon)

the afternoon is making a poem of itself

the sunlight pours on the land like honey

(the sunlight lies on the land like a tender regard)

this is the afternoon (a time for music)

sun, the sunlight is the (music) the music the music (the music) the music (the music) the music the music

of (this time) of the a(fter-noon)

the sunlight pours itself on the land and lies on the land like a tender regard

they stand about and wait for the boat,

they wait for the boat, the kanaris, to come in . . .

APRIL 14/64   (AFTERNOON)

the town keeps changing (everything does). one part looks like the center, and then another, then another: what looked like the center at one point, becomes the outskirts now; what seemed to be the zippiest part of the crowd, may be after all the most stagnant . . .

one thing i've seen and have meant to mention: that at the bottom of the social ladder, victimized often, and looked on (with pity and fear) by all, are the divers . . .

the fishermen (who are really the salt of the earth) think the divers have chosen badly . . .

the mechanics (who accompany the sponge-boats) are paid less, but are proud of their skill (and its relative sanctions) . . .

the captains are captains . . .

those who have a business in town, have a business . . .

only the divers are thought to be (practically without a skill) ("it takes only ten minutes to learn," said captain nicos) (with a very temporary hold on health and an even more transitory hold on money) courageous (if not merely lacking in the wisdom it takes to avoid great danger) . . .

they are the bottom rung of the social ladder (as close to the floor of this sea as the sponges they dive for) but they are also (in some sense) the heroes of the town . . .

they are, after all, what gives it its existence: no sponge, no captain, no sponge, no clipper, no sponge, no seller, and so, no town . . .

the divers are encouraged to spend money before they've been paid; the merchants lend it to them at exorbitant rates; and so the town grows on clippings and on usury . . .

and thus they are victimized (on land and sea); it doesn't occur to them to organize; they respond to a challenge which is beyond the considerations of security.

the sea calls (the sea, with its riches: the sea with its promise of life or death), the sea calls (and they from their dream-world answer): the sea calls to them: and they plunge in . . .

what are the riches of the sea to a man half-idiot? the riches of the sea are light and greenery: an aqueous vision: the treasure of sponge . . .

they are driven to wrest their lives from the sea, and (coming ashore) to lose them again; stand dripping to see them taken away . . .

APRIL 11/64   ST MACARIUS

talked with nicos (the captain who speaks good italian) and he told me more about sponge-diving. (even with his good italian there was a lot i missed.) he confirmed what others had told me about the general routine: each diver goes down at the most three times a day, is spelled by others. the rest of the time he lies around (probably in his bunk and not on the deck and this for the following reasons:) if he's gone down, says the captain, and it hasn't gone right, then within a half hour or so, he gets black and blue marks on his skin, probably around his hips. these marks (if light) are warning signs and not the actual symptoms of paralysis. if he even imagines that he has them, though, he is checked over by the captain, and if he has is laid off for the day. by the next day (if he's careful at this point) he can go back to work. but if he disregards them, and goes for another deep dive on that same day, says the captain, it could kill him. so the signs are very important: for this reason lying around on deck is no good: sunburn or a deep tan would tend to camouflage the signs. for the same reason, smoking a cigarette as soon as you get out of the water is thought to be good: nicotine has an effect on the blood which brings out the black and blue faster and with more definition (though i'd think if it had that much effect it ought to be avoided for a while). on the contrary, he says, at this point it's a medicine.

michali who sells peanuts yelled to me from his stand to come over a minute. said i had chalk on the back of my jacket (from leaning against back wall in this evening's crowded movie-house) dusted it off a little with his hand & let me join the crowd (well-dressed) in the evening promenade. but an old man standing next to him said he hadn't finished the job & made him call me back for another try. this time he asked if i had a handkerchief in my pocket. he took it, rubbed again harder, then said it was good enough, till i could do it myself in the morning, & let me go.

another man, 60, but feeling old, corrected a couple of my greek expressions. & when i repeated them to him correctly, reached out to embrace me.

& stavros (of the royal fishing family) said with tremendous seriousness: my father likes you very much.

OCTOBER 27/68

i asked michali, a fisherman, who has been married a year & has just had a son, how his children were. child, i corrected myself. child, he assented to my correction. he's little, he said, showing me with his hands & turning down the corners of his mouth, as though the son were a fish of unsatisfactory size. we tried taking him out today in his cart (said michali) but the weather's not good (he pointed with four or five fingers to the sky) & he's really too small . . .

a carriage, i said, has he got a carriage? yes, said michali, a present from my father . . .

one distinguished-looking old man in the fishing section has everything: a captain's cap (penetrating brown eyes, a rudder nose) walrus moustache, a droop-stemmed pipe, a string of enormous amethyst worry-beads & a thick loop-handled (round-handled) cane.

he looks as though he was born for it all: as though it had all been invented for him.

his five-year-old grandson (named basili, or king) seems fully pre-
pared to grow into it all.

NOVEMBER 3/68

when kurt helmholtz first arrived on the island he was enchanted by
its beauty. "so spare," he wrote. "the rocks glower over the sea like
the locks of wotan."

mrs. finch-asbury began her column: "the young men dance all night;
even the old men are tireless."

portia birmingham wrote: "dear mums: we've been here three days
& really there's nothing to do."

NOVEMBER 5/68

four little girls walk down the road hand-in-hand. a motorcycle comes
up behind them and frightens them into calling each other names . . .

———

the face of one single being
after another:

the face of the island

———

an island
that looks
out to sea

& looks out
to sea

& looks out
to sea . . .

———

the face of one
waiting & waiting

waiting & waiting

waiting for a
good he knows
he cannot
make

JULY 17/69   KALYMNOS

this is in the house used for typing.
another, up overlooking the sea, for sleeping.
another, up overlooking a grove, for writing (with the sea far off, but
visible).

house for typing noisiest. when typing hear no noise. when not, so
much one does not want to begin. what noise: metalwork shop just
three houses away: bang bang bang.

carpenter shop even closer: electric band saw, other mechanical saws
& sounds.

the gri gri boys (fishing crews) have just left, off on a windy sea; maybe
back before midnight to stagger around, drink a *coupa*, large glass of
retsina, & early to bed.

every afternoon the captains & crew sit at tables under a tree, outside
of evdokia's cafe, or under another, outside of angeli's, drink coffee
(small cups of turkish) or lemonades, & make what seem to be the same
old jokes with each other, but which probably change slightly from
day to day. they sit all afternoon from three to six, watching the sea,
waiting for the captains, or even for one captain to decide whether
the weather is good enough to start out in. then, near six, each cap-
tain gives a signal to his crew & they scramble for their places. they're
not allowed to be late or absent (or they're docked in their pay) so they
all stick together, by the waterfront, through the day.

most of the fishermen (these) come from a village on kos, the island directly across from kalymnos, an hour and a half away by fast caïque, and visible from the kalymnos waterfront. most of them have spent many summers at these same cafes, so they are not really strangers, but they are not, on the other hand, at home; this is not their island; it doesn't even have their island's (fairly cool, but humid) climate, and their families are not here. they sit all day, looking both at the sea, & at their island home.

or they play cards, one with the other, in the dark, & sometimes cool, cafe (angeli's), for small, small stakes (like a cup of coffee).

the crews dress raffishly, but with a certain decorum, & each man has his style. most are barefooted, though some wear sandals, usually the heavy-soled plastic kind. almost all wear caps: a wide variety. all dress lightly, but have sweaters stowed away against windy nights.

JULY 19/69

have moved the whole prose-show into the poems house: what will come, poems or jrnl? poems or prose?

poems house is up in hills beyond hill-village, chora. rented from sick nervous crafty pain-ridden old lady who in the end came up with a good deal, cleaned house, fitted it out with pail for the well, cup for the pail, a medal of Theotokos, & a lamp for night.

(i went to see her in athens; then she came to kal to make this deal: about $50 a year for a nice solid house on hillside outside village.)

the hill-house has a well, on the raised concrete porch outside the front door; i've drawn some water from it in the shiny new corrugated (iron?) pail, and scooped out a little in the dark blue plastic (white inside) cup the landlady brought for me. i use it mostly to rinse my mouth or gargle & have swallowed so far (in all these days) only a little.

other phenomena: this afternoon when i came into the poems hut, i noticed on the table where clean paper was stacked (blank, ready for poems) a fairly large rat turd (rat, i think, not mouse) had been deposited, just one, square in the middle of the top sheet. concrete poem.

no visible animals in the hut but a few, fairly large, red ants.

olive trees i write about are nodding in the wind: wind that's currently ruffling the sea & will probably keep the gri gris home again, on shore to drink (despondently enough, since all are now broke) or to see another movie they've all seen before.

drink: not drink. most of the gri gri crew will just go to the show.

(like circus roustabouts) they are strangers & familiar, familiar & strange, wherever they go.

dimitrios the cop asks about my writing methods. i write poems in pencil & copy them on the typewriter. prose i write directly on the typewriter. what are the poems about? nature, i say: what i see of the hills & sky. now i'm beginning to write prose: about myself, a journal, what i see & feel from day to day. you're beginning to write about yourself, he asks. yes, i say. that's good too, he says (as he gets out of the community taxi at his stop).

two wise kids came by the other day: one from the west, and one from ethiopia: john (the west) & theodore—who's partly greek, but born in ethiopia & looks like the princely son of haile selassie.

they stopped at the typing house and read the scrolls of poems i had there: theodore read most, saying he didn't like poetry usually but did like these & saw what i'd meant when i'd said the day before that i was working on a new kind. both boys (they're about 27 & 24) said that even then they'd pictured something like this they now saw. i asked theodore if he got tired reading & he said no—the rhythm mostly, but also the simple and natural words (words referring to the natural scene) & the repetitions kept him going. said something like this takes place in african music: that the important thing for a drummer or dancer, for example (singer too), is to get to the very center of the rhythm, center of the beat, "the nerve," said theodore, of the rhythm: to find that first: to start from it as a base, and from it all other things, even very elaborate things, develop.

which sounded like african music, like hindu music too, but also like bach.

the captains i like, & the people in general are those who seem to have found that center; it is not that they are either "good" or "bad": it is rather that they are fully alive, fully themselves, & that they, again the "best" of them, seem to have gone through a baptism (of not just water: of fire as well) from which there is no turning back.

i don't know whether my friend fat manoli has (really got) this quality or not

but i know that his old captain sdrega has, a quality that shows in every move (& in every picture you take of him).

satori probably isn't the word for it.

it has little (consciously, at least) to do with the sparklings of inner peace, though that may be at the matrix of this visible strength. but "peace," philosophic peace, is scarcely a thing that a man on this (generally) embattled island would consciously strive for; he would aim rather to be a man, to be himself; to be a good captain, perhaps, if he is a captain; or even, somewhere in the back of his mind, a good kalymnian.

stellio, when i asked him once quite confidentially, how he thought i was doing with the community here (fishing community particularly), all of whom say they like me, answered fine, just fine, but no one, absolutely no one knows what you're doing, and everyone wonders why you stay so long & what your work could be like. i told them i've been to your house a number of times & i can see what you do: you write poems and take pictures sometimes. i tell them, but none of them knows what to think.

i guess it does (to them) seem surprising that a man would come and like the island so much that he would not only not easily leave it, but would make a positive effort to stay.

& why would he spend so much time by himself: writing—writing what? & taking pictures, so many, sometimes of one man. & never of merchants or doctors, as far as i know, but fishermen, fishermen, fishermen, fishermen, fishermen.

everyone in town, especially those who listen to the radio, talking about the men on the moon. everyone is proud of "the americans" & of one (at least conjectural) kalymnian who was part of the team of scientists that worked on the project.

many kalymnians said at first "i don't think the Lord will let them land"—but most of the modern types, like george the printer, who's been to australia, & panioyotis vouros, 15, who runs the candy store & is modern by nature, felt that this was a silly attitude.

perhaps they see my being here as though this is the moon & i am an astronaut, and now that i've come here & written a little & photographed a little, they wonder why i don't go back to my planet, the earth.

it is true that a greek community is a community, & anyone who isn't part of it, what is he part of?

they say: you'll get to be a real kalymnian: you'll get married and raise a family here.

then i would be part of the community, and then they'd understand why i stay.

they describe me as an "isichos anthropos"—a peaceful man.

& for this they seem to like and respect me.

if i were always causing a fuss they'd soon enough run me off the island.

this isn't an island of tourists: it is an island of kalymnians.

have i caused any fusses? i don't really think so. any at all? i don't think one.

but i've done a few odd things: i must have lived in twenty houses, really, twenty at least, in the six years i've been here.

how many years?
5 or 6.

when did i come here? spring 1964.
what is it now? summer 1969.

where were you last year? from oct 1967 to oct 1968 (about) i was in america.

how many years then, actually on the island?
4 or 5.

even now how many houses are you "living in" at once?

3: one up in hagios stephanos: fishing section high & right over the sea, where i sleep, eat breakfast & do most living things (collect my laundry, do some; store books & blankets).

second: down in town: where i type: this is the one that has all the noises: metal-work, mama & child.

third: up. outside the hill-village, where i write, mostly poetry, but now, too, this jrnl.

JULY 22/69

almost as soon as i open the door of the hill-house, i roll the paper into the machine & bang bang bang

talk somewhat to journal all through the day, knowing that most of what i say won't actually go into it: that i'll write whatever i write once i start writing. & that no whole subject probably will ever be covered. some attempt maybe to lay out in dotted lines a range of the spectrum. spectrum of what? spectrum if only of my worries. & joys? yeah, yeah, & of my joys.

sometimes, i have conversations with an imaginary guru, naturally one who lives inside me. he used to be a psychiatrist: at least in the old days a lot of my conversations were started with, & a lot of my problems heard out or resolved by, an imaginary viennese who listened carefully, often accusingly, & showed me with a few apt technical phrases how far i had erred in my thinking, or behavior. the viennese fellow has disappeared; comes back if ever for very short visits; but has been replaced by chuang tzu (sometimes merton, or sometimes chuang tzu in merton translation) who tells me other wisdoms: usually the wisdoms of abstinence & avoidance; of retreat, prayer & preparation, of non-attachment, of "sitting quietly doing nothing," of seeking smallness, not greatness, or of seeking nothing at all.

as i don't think i really understood the "psychiatrist" half of the time, i'm not sure i really understand "chuang tzu." i respect him though, don't resent him, as i often did the psychiatrist; feel that he knows i don't know but that little by little there'll be things i can learn. i picture him with shaved head, a listener (& yet a practical man), a listener who appreciates, a listener with humor; a storehouse—but very light storehouse—of wisdom; made like modern electronic ears of light, light materials, but of great receiving strength.

what he promotes is wisdom, what he promises is grace. zen wisdom, perhaps; zen grace, but certainly wisdom & grace.

one feels that all philosophies, zen, & yoga are ways of approaching wisdom & "enlightenment"—they are ways of approaching an enlightened state in which one's behavior is always or almost always "spontaneously" right.

to be "enlightened" is not to shine; nor to bring multitudes to the hill where one sits cross-legged, to listen.

it is rather to know what one is doing (& even, perhaps, to enjoy it).

thus i am glad that they say i am "isichos" & not that they say i am rich (which i'm not).

they've discerned a direction i've taken, and one which i hope i shall keep to.

sometimes i've tried to see more than i saw (and have tried to forget what i've seen).

& sometimes i've tried to see less than i saw (& have tried to forget what i've seen).

but the world here is whole: whole & large & patient. the longer i stay, the more patiently i seek, the more, i believe, i shall learn.

here comes the shepherd
& his flock

(out of the shadow
of the rock)

it must be one thing to imagine what a guru is like, another to see
one. seeing merton was little enough like seeing an imaginary guru.

yet he had one quality, particularly in the last years, but even (to a large
degree) from always, from even before he (formally) became a catho-
lic: a certainty of tread.

that might sound as though he plonk plonk plonked like a german
soldier as he walked down the street. actually, he didn't: he danced
(danced almost like fred astaire: bang bang bang; or bojangles
robinson, tappety bam bam bam) but he knew where he was dancing.

he did walk with joy. he walked explosively: bang bang bang. as
though fireworks, small, & they too, joyful, went off every time his
heel hit the ground.

this was true when he was still in college. it was true when he was
just out of college, and it was true the last time i saw him bang bang
banging down a long hallway at the monastery. he walked with joy:
knew where he was going.

first time i noted how he walked was on fifth avenue, near the park,
in spring (late afternoon, i guess) as he came from somewhere uptown
to meet me. bang bang bang. & that time i thought about fred astaire.

did merton & i make any resolutions as young men? one (& it wasn't
tacit) was to talk simply. merton certainly succeeded in that, & got a
lot said in simple (not simplistic) language.

after merton became a catholic, was living & teaching at st. bona-
venture's, and was being fed good soups by the nice german nuns there,
he was more determined to write simply, and about simple things:
things they could understand & that would help them in their lives.

JULY 26/69

eustathios, the church-step beggar, has gone away: got sick and was sent off to athens (by the authorities). he wasn't always a beggar, but he was always badly disabled. when i first came here he was still working as a kind of town crier, and crier of boats. he would drag himself, walking on one leg, it seemed, and dragging the other down the main street of town & along by the sea announcing the names and schedules, the ports of call of the boats that would arrive that day and the next. he sang or chanted this information in a heartbreaking voice as though ninevah, ninevah were falling. we asked a hotel landlady once if he were paid (by the travel agencies) to do this work & to sing thus. she said no: they pay him not to, but he does it anyway.

during the last year or two they must have stopped paying him not to, and he stopped doing it, too. perhaps could not even walk that far. he sat on the stoop in front of the church every day, just sat there; and people would give him whatever they could.

JULY 29/69

the woman who lives in the house at the bottom of the hill asked me with a great warm smile how i was doing; i said fine, and that i was going to work. good, she said, tapping her head, or something, to show that the work i meant was intellectual.

which perhaps it is: feels more, the way i do it, like adam naming the plants & animals. looking & naming: not doing very much more.

i keep thinking that i'll write something about how the town keeps changing & changing & changing. according to my moods, according to its seasons; according to its moods and according to actual physical changes: who comes, who goes, who's born & who dies, what buildings are put up & what torn down.

it changes spiritually too: its whole tone changes, sometimes from day to day & greatly from season to season.

i think i should talk sometime about how when a stranger comes into the harbor it looks like the harbor of a doll's town: doll's houses of various colors, small and square, all around the basin of hills that forms the harbor; the half-moon of hills; little houses brightly colored. anyone of romantic mind wants to disembark here immediately, though it's seldom on anyone's itinerary. & when you've lived here a while it sometimes still seems like a doll's town: a town of little people, living full lives, but in miniature. this littleness does not refer to their stature, since many kalymnians are tall, and many quite broad, but rather to the compactness of the whole: the feeling that so many condimensions of a whole & real world are contained in after all very little space. most of the life of the island is concentrated in the town, and in a few other centers: small, half-villages at logical points in the topography. but there are also comparatively vast uninhabited spaces; so that in this, too, it is like a continent (a small, small continent); like america—with new york here, san francisco there (chicago, more or less, in the middle) and many wide spaces between.

as a child i had a recurrent fantasy of watching a miniature town (or was it a circus?) that lived under water—that lived, now i remember, under "waterglass"—a miniature world, that was a circus. i would watch it in the morning, when the performers, waking up, would come out of their tents and caravans and do all their daily tasks, washing their clothes, hanging them out to dry, cooking; taking baskets to go shopping. since it was all taking place under water, or under waterglass, in the bright light of a summer morning, when the acrobats, or their wives, for example, would wring out the clothes they had washed, what would come from them, into the morning atmosphere, would not be drops of water, but bubbles of air.

i have often remembered the little community, the underwater circus, since coming to the island.

it's certainly true that some of the people i like best in town (though i've never known any of them very well) are a few (are there 10?) small, compact fishermen types, some old, some young: each almost perfect in his way. (i like to photograph them): i like to watch them walk, or sit & mend nets, or fish, or swim; (one even rides a motorcycle well: i saw him learn)—or hop onto a boat or off one (all the fishermen do that well); but best of all: to walk (as though over water), or to sit mending nets (as though to sit forever). a kind of perfection that beats the (schooled) equilibrium of the japanese. or leave the japanese out of it: say simply a kind of perfection.

greeks, just the same, have classical ideas of beauty: to be considered really good-looking you must be of a certain size & good proportions, have regular features, graceful bearing, and all the other attributes of venus & adonis.

mark van doren: when a boat-master out at the shipyard saw his picture, he said: who's he? he looks so simple: he looks as though he might be a sponge-diver.

AUGUST 5/69

sometimes it seems as though the island were a school of thought; as though there were living, somewhere in the mountains, an invisible zen-master who kept everyone on the beam. if you walk along in dark thoughts (down the main street) no one will say hello to you, or if they do, they say it timidly, knowing not only that it would be wrong to interrupt you now, but even to recognize you as a visible being when you were not (as they usually manage to be) in your full fine feeling. but if you are feeling very well, they say hello with joy.

on such a day, someone may run over spontaneously & shake your hand.

the joy i am talking about, the full fine feeling, in greek is called *kefi*. some days you have *kefi* & some you don't. when you do, you are full of spontaneous good actions, every one of which may be expected to turn out right.

confidential report: four boys just out of school have found what sounds like an archaeological treasure in a cave somewhere outside of town. getting to it involves some undersea work, the cave being half in the water: sounds like a fairly important find, not only archaeologically but numismatically: pirate treasure. (also, of course, sounds like fantasy, but there have been some important finds here on the island in the past few months.) the boys (for every reason but those of safety) are eager to keep the treasure to themselves: to dive for it, bring it up, piece by piece and item by item by item (a big job, it sounds like), hide it all somewhere, and then, by whatever means presents itself, take it out of the country and sell it abroad. all of this would have to be done secretly, and would take, i think, tremendous talent for clandestine activity. legally, what they should do is report the find to the police since all such treasure, all antiquities found in the earth or under the sea, by law belongs to the government. & the government is jealous of its rights. already, say the boys, they've been followed by the police in the direction of the cave. (they're almost sure to be caught up with before they've even removed a coin.) two months ago some small (9-year-old) boys who reported—or eventually re-ported—a treasure, which may only have been a dream, were taken to the police station, slapped and pushed around and told that they'd have their tongues cut out if they didn't tell all they knew about it.

i told my one acquaintance among the four to forget all about the treasure and to swim in some other part of the island; but he's not likely to do that either. "we have our futures to think about," he said, "& we'll do what we can."

AUGUST 21/69

Wisdom (Under water)

as the life of the body is made up of many elements in lively motion and lively interchange (and in strict but deeply mysterious order) so is the life of the town.

exchanges are made by words and gestures, even, most importantly, by glances: life imparted from one being to another: given without loss, but taken with gain. given & taken (& ready to give again).

as the living body, whole body, out & in, has a texture, so has the life of the town. a tone & a texture, changing from moment to moment & yet in many aspects remaining the same.

this is the texture of life, a texture that is woven as closely as on a continent, and as closely on a rock (with one living man) as on an island.

it is to perceive this texture that we have seeing eyes, hearing ears and feeling hands. it is not only to be warned by it of dangers, nor invited by it to desire, but to enjoy, to appreciate it from moment to moment in its life and in its passing.

our contact with life, with the flow of life, is a physical contact: spiritual, too—but physical none the less.

to touch life, to know life, we must somehow bang into it: though if we stand off it, it will come, & grasp us.

i swam again today. clear water. slow-moving shadows over the rocks. the rocks themselves not white or grey: more pink & white; blue & grey. a strange man, gardener, comes and swims too: scrambles lithely over the rocks and undresses behind one. naked swimmer, washing the dust of the garden, he says, from a thin & muscular brown and white body. looks amphibious, even on land, and most at home in the water.

the undersea vision, even at shallow depths, is almost narcotic. whatever is seen is seen with such peace, such composure. to look thus wide-eyed at all phenomena would surely be a kind of joy, a kind of psychic nourishment. we glide above objects, seeing them through glass, through the heavy, light-charged water: fallen rocks are the walls of a valley: below them a sleeping plain of smooth, white sand.

sea calls to the blood, waking those members farthest removed from the heart to a new circulation: the blood within, the brine without, calling to each other as day to night, as night to day.

a feeling, experienced by all the old men who swim daily, of being reborn in the sea.

and they are shaped, licked like bear-cubs by their mother, and they issue from a summer of sea remade.

the undersea vision may (in fact) be a foetal vision: full of dim light, full of bright, if far off, hope.

my buttocks were limp: they are getting firmer: my pectorals non-existent: they are shaping up. i begin to feel more like a man, like a creature: less like a disembodied soul.

i like to swim with the little old men: there are now two who are almost alike, who swim for the same seven minutes about, climb out, saying "that's enough for today"—"a little, and good," dry themselves quietly in the sun & leave.

"little, old"—they are only ten years older than i, but have a thousand years of experience ahead of me.

to be wise is to know, for one thing, which way the wind blows . . .

knowing how to stay alive & healthy (well-fed & with adequate air and sleep) in all kinds of conditions is also a part of wisdom

the wisdom of survival.

wisdom for survival.

he who is imbued with the wisdom of survival is not only fit for "survival" himself, but for teaching it to others. (even to generations of others.)

"the survival of the fittest"—not of the fiercest, not of the fastest—the fittest, among men, may, after all, be the wisest.

not every place in the world, at every time and in every condition would be a good school for wisdom. but wisdom is a "culture" (as yoghurt is) and where it begins to grow it develops regularly. wise generations, for a while at least, follow the generations of the wise.

wisdom and moderation certainly have something to do with each other. he who does not know how to moderate an action (to moderate, in fact, all his actions) cannot be wise.

pan metron ariston say the greeks: every good thing in measure. (wise words from the ancients.)

not too little, and not too much: the meaning of moderation.

most refusals to do this or that, to eat or drink this or that, in greece, have to do with moderation: the observance of a clearly perceived (if seldom verbalized) inner law.

to live among greeks (and especially, perhaps, among kalymnians) is to live in an atmosphere of wisdom.

where among kalymnians is the greatest degree of wisdom to be observed? i think, almost certainly, among the fishermen.

what are the wise things they say and the wise things they do? only by living among them, watching them carefully, listening attentively can one learn from them gradually.

learn to be a fisherman? learn, slowly, to be wise.

to live among wise people is to learn wisdom gradually. can wisdom be learned? can all men learn wisdom? i think almost all men can gain somewhat in wisdom and can gain more in wisdom by living among the wise.

for wisdom is a language, and he would learn something of their language. he might not learn to use it with great ability, but every year for a while he would learn a little, if by nature, he was incapable of learning more.

what is the value of wisdom? many values, but perhaps the most obvious, the most nearly tangible: the value of survival.

is survival, too, a matter of dubious value? it may be for some. (i doubt that it is for the wise.)

AUGUST 25/69 (ANYWAY, MONDAY)

house-moving again: seem to be slipping out of one & into another. downtown. both of them. i'm moving, that is, from the typing-house with all the bang-bang to another that may do for winter as a "house."

winter, anyway, in the air. still hot in late august, but days getting shorter at both ends.

(in olean, now, late in august, there'd be winter-fall fogs on the mountain and lake-roads, late at night.)

a wedding last night (at the home of anthony tsougranis's daughter-in-law) where were several old friends. the presence of pavlos kourounis (presence & absence) was felt by us all: we told a few jokes and remembered him.

& walking home later at night i remembered him clearly. did i wish he was still on earth? (who knows what to wish?)

in one sense, i guess, he had suffered enough, and had gone, even cheerfully enough, to his rest.

(but he was sad to die, sad to leave us, and we were sad to have him go.)

talking of death as a kind of rest is probably another big euphemism. rest is when you take a nap & wake up again feeling great.

thinking about jesus and "do you believe in jesus?"—i believe i do. i believe, at least (i believe i believe) in what he believed in. "do you believe he's alive now and sitting at the right hand of God"? i believe at least that he got where he was going, and that where he was going is exactly where i should like to go.

our identity is bound with our memories: wash away memory and identity disappears . . .

only to appear again with our next action.

i remember the people i loved (who have died) or who've just disappeared—remember their traits as though it were a sacred duty.

what possible use for all those memories unless we were (somehow) all to meet again?

LUNCH WITH THE FISHERMEN   KALYMNOS

up and out early this morning (in time to be drinking tea at an outside table of a fishermen's cafe before the radio went on at seven. it starts with a kind of muezzin call on a trumpet. then comes three or four minutes of a baritone orthodox priest intoning the liturgy. this stops and the boisterous national anthem begins. then about fifteen minutes of pretty sillysounding gymnastics—the teacher who lives in my house bounces along with them every morning in the kitchen as he washes—and then the news. the crowd on the terrace (and on all the terraces of greece) listens seriously to this (seriously and calmly), digesting all the facts and storing them for conversation later in the day (adding them as well to the great oral tradition that has been handed down since the days of pericles)).

then i walked down to where the fishermen come in, to where women stand outside and stretch the first strands for a carpet, to where the girl in the hut was already at work on a new rug for the day (she was pleased with some pictures i took of her and wants me to do some others of her mother).

then other errands (the post office and pictures a man on a boat will take back to kos to have printed); after as much running around as i could think of i got back to the house too early to work: the landlady was in my room (in everyone's room) and cleaning up the place; i wandered out a little disconsolately, thinking if there's one thing i know about greece it's not to be out in the street at eleven in the morning. i didn't feel like sitting in another cafe; there are no parks; there was hardly another place to sit: i went to the fishermen's wharf, sat down on a blue cement stanchion, took my (pocket-sized) grammar book out of my pocket, and began to look through it. someone called me (or whistled) from the pier behind me. (i don't know how i knew it was for me, but) i looked around. a small boy was gesturing for me to come. somebody smiled, a bright smile from one of the boats, but i didn't know who. as i got closer, i recognized mikali from the good boat at kos. i ran across the gangplank (which is a simple plank and still feels to me like a tightrope), shook hands with mikali and the others, and sat down. what was i doing here? was kalymnos good, they asked me? yes, but kos is better, huh? (mikali comes from kalymnos but is married now to a girl from kos and lives there.) where's costa? in town: his wife lives here. where's manoli? he's wandering around; he'll be back. i'll go and get him, said one of the kids, and shot off. how long have you been here? a couple of weeks: when did *you* get here? just today. when are you going back to kos? tomorrow.

the kid came back, and in a little while manoli did too: the same amble. he was wearing a red shirt today, and the cap: no sweaters: a pair of (heavy) rubber boots. he waved the same light wave from the pier and shook hands when he got across the gangplank. he and mikali sat down on the deck, but when i tried to do that too, mikali got me one of the little stools that are always around. more talk back and forth about what everyone had been doing. where's the captain? he's in kos. sick. (mikali suggested by lifting his thumb several times to his lips that he had been drinking too much.) manoli said, he's not at his house, but he's sick.

they asked again where i was from, what i was doing here, when i would be going back to france. when i go back to france i should write them a card said mikali.

maybe i could invite them to lunch, i was thinking (but how can i invite them all?).

will you stay here and have lunch with us? asked manoli. stay and have lunch. sure, i'd like to. (when he gets back to france, he'll be able to say he had lunch on a boat with some fishermen, manoli said happily to the others.)

is it ready yet, asked manoli; not yet, said mikali;
cook it well (it's beans), explained mikali.

when it was ready, we went around and sat on what i guess is the hatch (they did: manoli brought my stool around for me). spread out were two large white basins full of rich bean soup—lots of beans and red soup—tomatoes and olive oil—the national dish, said mikali (and it is)—loaves of bread, and another basin full of olives. one basin (really a basin) full of soup was meant for me: the other, only slightly larger, was for all of them; six soup spoons were laid around the edges of their basin: one spoon leaned against the rim of mine. mikali sliced bread and handed it to me; i passed it to manoli; the others seemed to be taking care of themselves.

manoli crossed himself (lightly) without seeming to; the others didn't, without not seeming to, and we began to eat. the soup was wonderful, and they all thought so too. one of the boys brought mikali a little envelope full of pepper. do you want some, he asked me. no thanks. he poured a little into the community basin. then a little more. manoli said that was about enough; but someone else said (joking) to put it all in; so mikali (joking) put it all in. they stirred it up and ate it that way, laughing. it's always like this, said mikali. no fights, said manoli (we're like brothers).

i then went into a speech i had heard from somebody else: that fishermen were all good types, never fought, could even drink hard and never fight—that indeed they were the people of the Lord. No one picked up on it very much, though manoli made the best he could of it: they don't fight, he said. then when he heard about the drinking, he said: they don't drink very much. drinking's no good. if you drink, you can't work. (it's bad for your stomach for one thing, and) you get sleepy.

earlier he had said that sponge-diving was no good either (no sir, not for him): he told me about how deep they go and pointed to his legs about the danger. they get some money, but it isn't worthwhile. this is a calm life (fishing) and a good one; (you don't get much, but) you can live.

it was a cool day even at noon; the sun came down on the boat just right through the net that was hanging up to dry. where were they going tonight? kephalo (the village in kos manoli was born in), a long trip from here: three hours. if the weather is good, we'll go on to kos (the town); if not, we'll come back here. they've got a lot of fish around kephalo (they haven't many around kos—which is why this is practically the only boat that goes out from there). you'll get them in these nets, i say (yeah). there are only a few weeks more of this fishing; after that it's against the law. then we'll go out in small boats (and catch little fish). manoli and yorgo will go out together then. (where was yorgo at this point? out at some cafe.)

while i talked to manoli, mikali talked to the boy who couldn't speak. mikali explained to me that he couldn't speak but was very bright and understood everything that went on (the boy—about twenty-four—then nodded and smiled in agreement); manoli gave me his version of the story: that from the time the boy's mother had had him, he couldn't speak, and if you spoke to him in the ear, he couldn't hear you.

(manoli comes on so much like the sea (so much like the sea on a very calm day) that whatever he announces, whatever he says, sounds like the proclamation of good news.)

(i couldn't eat all they had given me, and they couldn't eat all they had given themselves.) we poured the contents of my basin into theirs (once they were convinced i wasn't fooling). manoli had already crossed himself (at the end of the meal) and was leaning on one elbow still talking. the others had gone up to the prow, though mikali remained. a boy came on to the boat (wistfully) selling ice cream from a circular freezer he carried. a couple of boys up front bought some, and i offered to get some for manoli and mikali, but they said no. (we wanted to do this for you. but now if you pay us—) manoli explained it as though he were talking to his child.

mikali then said he'd have to go to sleep for a little while but i should stay and talk to manoli.

manoli had better go to sleep too, i said. not yet, said manoli. we can go for a little walk. mikali went below to his bunk, and we went (over the gangplank again) to the pier. as we walked down it to the town, yorgo came along, looked at me, then at manoli, and smiled: manoli! he said; manoli's good, he told me.

he walked along with us for a way (not quite in, not quite out of the group; i didn't know how or when to pull him in, thought perhaps manoli would). in a moment or two, however, the dormouse faded; cut off to the right: hardly a good-bye between them, just half a glance.

manoli and i walked on in the sun, down along the quay (the sea-cap, red shirt, and rubber boots suddenly looking fine and unique in the town).

shall we have some coffee, i asked him. sure, said manoli, we can stop in here (the nearest place: a table, an awning, two comfortable canvas-backed chairs).

how do you like it, i said, *vari glicko?* (this means very sweet (heavy with sugar): all the good-natured types i know prefer it this way. i like it *sketto*: no sugar at all.)

no, you have coffee, i'll have lemonade.

don't you drink much coffee? i asked.

not much, just at home (in the morning)—no coffee, no cigarettes, no drinking. i want my children to be strong. i need the money for food. i can't spend it on cigarettes and wine.

you're a good man, i said.

he laughed.

the kid had come for the order. do you want coffee? he said. no, lemonade (couldn't fight it). two lemonades, manoli said. don't have any, said the boy. what now? (should we get up and leave?) manoli said: two coffees, *vari glicko*.

i like it sweet, he said; my wife makes it sweet, and then i put more sugar on top of that.

when it came, we tasted it, and it wasn't so sweet after all. (someone out there had made it *metrio*.) more talk, about his family (has three sons) and then about yorgo. (his wife lives here, he said, but she's no good. she's sick? no, she's no good. she goes out with four other men. (takes all his dough.) if he says anything to her about anything, she's rough. he's scared of her. he's small. one time she said something to manoli, and he told her off. ever since then she's been as sweet as pie. how are you, she says; how's your wife? how are your kids? that's just the way yorgo ought to treat her, but he won't.)

i'd like to go out on the boat some night, i said for the five-thousandth time.

yes, he said (as he, and they all, always had), some night when it's very smooth.

not tonight, i guess, i suggested (looking at the tiny waves the wind was making).

not tonight, he agreed, but maybe tomorrow; if we go to kos, you come with us (more good news).

suddenly he said addio: i'll have to go and sleep for a while. got up and shook my hand.

i got up too and walked with him a little way down the street. you won't go to sleep? he said.

yes, i'll go to sleep for a little while too.

yes. go to sleep for a little while, then work.

another addio, and he walked to the boat.

i did sleep a little, and worked a little, and suddenly couldn't say any more. walked down to the pier and was just in time to see him pulling out for kephalo.

OCT 3/69   PATMOS

patmos, holy patmos. i've never come here without the feeling, at least on the first few days, that the island is holy.

the bend of the walk around the bay. the view of the monastery up on the hill (a citadel) as seen from far end of the bay.

the terracing of the hill.

a feeling, real feeling, of peace in the air.

got here last night, went directly from boat to a hotel i knew, installed in a corner room.

i see a moth squashed on the wall. must have squashed it myself last night. first act on coming into the room. good business for character in horror movie. doesn't much horrify me when i do it. horrifies the moth. maybe horrifies the angels. thoughts like that then horrify me.

i think if jean genet can write in jail, i can write in a room like this.

writing bang bang makes me feel glad. i ought to do it more often. instead i resist all day long: taking walks, sitting and staring, lying and sleeping. (lying down, that is, not telling lies: too idle for that.)

i think it would be good to come up here for a month, enjoy the peace and quiet, the relatively inexpensive life, and get some writing done.

ah, he likes to write, likes to get writing done, likes to get things on paper . . .

sometimes he can hardly see why, but sometimes he does. getting experience—daily, day to day experience—on paper makes it more of an experience. breaks it into discrete particles and puts them back together again. lets him know where he is & what he is doing, and prepares him for whatever new thing comes along. gets him ready with his cups and categories to contain whatever new thing "falls from heaven."

it is always, always seems to him, like adam naming the animals: they come to him as unnamed creatures, undifferentiated—bear and eagle. he names them and they fly asunder.

children shout outside the window. they haven't half the volume, half the strength, the *zori* (force) of those in kalymnos. the women here, too, when they talk, do it in a softer way. they even have secrets: one calls to the other and they disappear into silence.

but kalymnos is a small city, bustling and unified. sun strikes it in a stronger way. the faces of all the people are more distinct, more active, more alive. the atmosphere is more nervous, more "dynamic." an employee of the kal electric company has been working here for two months and looks far more relaxed than he did in kalymnos. he says the people here are far more peaceful—not as smart and shrewd, he implied, as those on "our" island. i'm not sure he's a born kalymnian either.

am whistling (as i feed paper into the machine) an old bunny berrigan (vernon duke) tune: "i can't get started"—which i usually take for a sign that that's just what's happening—i'm delaying—not getting close to what i want ("to what my soul most deeply wants") to write about. or to do. to do right here as work on paper.

because yes—he likes to "write"—but to "do"—to do a particular thing—perhaps on paper (perhaps on canvas—perhaps in stone—perhaps, perhaps in a musical score)—a thing that will stand, a thing that will bear (that will sustain) repeated contemplation: a thing that will sustain long contemplation, and that will (in a "deep" enough way) reward the beholder.

(joy, then, it would be, to get started on, to progress in, and to complete such a work.)

wind outside and probably clouds. a little boat came over this morning with tourists from ikaria (an island four hours away—northwest (?))—across an almost always rough sea. i thought for a few minutes of going back with them this afternoon, decided not to; now i wonder if even they will start out in this kind of weather. the bay here is usually quiet, but i'm sure it is full of waves now. & the sea will be rough.

voices in the hall; (just as i thought) the tourists won't go back to ikaria tonight. some will stay in this hotel (they're all demanding more blankets); others maybe at a fancier place. this one's good enough, at 20 drachs (65 cents) a night.

siderako—88—who works bent over in his garden all day and was walking down the street at dusk (rocking down the street) with some fresh-pulled beets seemed really glad to see me, as i was to see him. his handshake at whatever 80-age he is, is like iron, like his name.

he eats bread and drinks a large glass of his own (home-pressed) sweet dark wine for breakfast every day (they tell me). seems fuller of life than almost anyone i've ever seen (since padre pio). & merton, last time i saw him, was much like both of them.

old men in the cafeneion asked me: what's the oldest country?
china, i started to say.
india? they asked (before i had said a word).
maybe india, i said.
china, said the cafe owner (a friend) sort of secretly to me.
china, i said. china it is.
china, said the old men. china & india. what comes after that, egypt?
probably egypt, i said.

(but i've been realizing) that there are lots of facts—probably all contained in world almanac—that i've never known or have forgotten.

a (fairly neurotic) young guy in kalymnos was asking me all about rockets to the moon, and i couldn't give him a single sure answer.

what "fuel" exactly & how do they take off? even having been to a couple of astronautical conferences (in athens & belgrade) didn't help.

lots of things (not just facts) i've either never known or have forgotten.

lots tossed out like ballast for ascent; but is the ascent in progress?

went out to georgia's house today where mama, georgia, chrisoula and another sister (francesca?) from australia gave me fava & salad and a boiled sweet potato for (hurried and unexpected) lunch, and took me through the neighborhood to look for houses. result of the search is that i'll probably stay at manoli gambiarakis's, which is nicer than all of them, better equipped and not much more expensive than some i saw that had nothing (but peace & quiet) to offer. nothing, meaning no water nearby, no light but a kerosene lamp (which might be ok): stone floors usually & bear-trap beds.

a walk this afternoon out on a (familiar) high road by the sea. beautiful, volcanic rocks at roadside: apocalyptic-looking: sculptured: more by a painter (giotto—or even el greco) than by a sculptor (who'd want to make them into men, not rocks); strange majesty, strange intimacy too—they talk in a familiar voice: apocalyptic presences. (someone who wrote to me last week at kal said "those stones (in greece) really speak." now i know what he means.)

and i felt all today as i did yesterday that peace, deep feeling of peace is here. that here is where i should stay at least for a while (& heal the nerve-ends), that here things would grow, things would speak. (kal, summoned to mind, seems a wild, wild merry-go-round from here.) that here the days would go as though nothing were happening, but something would be happening. that i would do nothing all day long, but toward the evening of every day i'd write (& slowly become) more articulate: almost every time i've been here the days have gone that way: i've felt as though nothing were happening; yet at the end of the year i've found that the work i did at patmos was (often) work that stood.

work: there's no doubt that keeping a journal is a little like talking to your doctor, and that sometimes it takes months even years to get a good stream of conversation going out to him.

there is always the underlying assumption that someone, even a well-knit someone, who knows what he wants & who lives inside you, wants to talk & has something to say; knows what it is he has to say, knows what he's seen and what exactly he wants to say about and in it and through it; but he waits, he waits for the moment (in which) he's sure he'll be heard: a moment in which he can speak without interruption.

he even knows that his work is that, that his role in the world, in the universe is that: (at some well-chosen point) to speak with fulsomeness & truth: to say, that is, what he sees; to say it wholely, clearly.

he does not come to speak about himself; if he speaks about himself he is trying or meaning to speak about the whole.

he speaks (the person inside us speaks) as though he were the oracle of delphi, not interested in which of two antagonists is listening: he only speaks the truth (as he hears it): he only speaks the truth as well as he can.

can he speak of meat hanging in the butcher's shop? can he see it as it is? can he see it as it's hanging? can he relate it (& should he not relate it?) to cattle on the hillside, to clouds in the sky?

wind, wind outside the window; the louvers are good: no draft in the room.

georgia's wonderfully earnest face: has a fleur-de-lys birthmark impressed in the flesh (as in sealing-wax) just below the right eye.

her mother a black-haired, black-eyed woman, continually hopped-up on coffee, loves me & i'm glad (would hate her to hate me).

their father died lately at 90: worked hard in his fields until the last half of this year. they loved him (so did i) but said the last months of his illness were "heavy" for them all.

they've recovered now, look well and fully alive: they showed me a lively, lively photo of him that had been taken by a swedish visitor, out in the field.

georgia asked his three-year-old grandson (named after him: michali) where he was. michali didn't know. show him (me) with your hand, said georgia, pointing as she felt, to the sky. michali raised his head and looked straight up, making an honest investigation of the ceiling.

mama's son yerasimos is a monk (& priest) at the monastery (the big citadel) on the hill. she does his laundry (as she knows she should) in a separate tub with separate water from that of the rest of the family. (a priest's clothes are sacred.) now she does someone else's from up there (if i understood her right) and for some reason he gets an even more separate tub. (if he tries getting his clothes washed in yerasimos's tub, she indicates, she'll have his scalp.)

mama (who was the old man's second wife) is much younger than he was. if he was 90, she is 54 & is the mother of 12 of his children, of whom yerasimos is the most favored. though he lives at the monastery, they also keep a nobly furnished room for him at the house.

yerasimos doesn't like fava (a kind of yellow mash grown on the hillsides here, and which everyone is expected to eat during Lent) and this is a disappointment to mama. i like it fine, and thus somehow fulfill her dream of having a whole & fava-eating son.

wild wind, i wonder if the big boat will come tomorrow.

OCTOBER 5/69, SUNDAY

walked out on the pier today and saw someone mending a net and looking at me from one of the caïques. a fellow-kalymnian. he and his brother fish deep for sponges with a huge heavy net. i didn't know his name, but knew his face. he had some (oldish) news for me: that yanaro (my friend yanni) is back from bengazi, and that lots of the other guys are, as well.

i saw him later (in the afternoon) dressed in style (sponge-diver style) a black shirt tucked smartly under his belt and walking with a (challenging) sponge-diver amble. "variarme" he said, "i get bored: walk here, walk there—there's no place to go." (a typical—and especially, spongy—reaction to patmos.) in kalymnos there are people, movement, something to do. patmians don't like it there, too hot for one thing, & too noisy; but they'll admit that it's nice to see a little movement (a few girls passing) just the same.

the sponge-diver's face (though he doesn't always dive) was thin, trim and lively, ruddy tan from sea and sun: it also looked somehow like a sponge—as though you could wring the sea-water from it.

he also looked livelier, shrewder, more laughing than a nice enough (earnest) patmian of about his same age (32–36) with whom he was standing and talking another time when i passed.

last night sat around a cafe-taverna run by a nice old friend from samos. two athenians were there, young workers, both engaged, with two others, in building a dam out at griko, a fair distance out, at the southern point of the island. they asked me if i'd drink some wine and poured me some, offered me cigarettes, too, and later coffee. one spoke a little english and liked to try. the other, from up around thessaloniki (by birth), told me about some nice villages near there and pointed them out to me on a map. said, too (both workers said), that these places were near mt athos (ayion oros) where there were many monasteries and where i could go and stay for two months if i liked for nothing. andreas, the one who told me first about the villages, said he had gone there often and stayed for a while. jakovos, the other (who's boss on the job), acted as though he had been there too: said the monks (at athos) were nice guys (not like the ones here who, he felt, had turned the monastery into a tourist attraction).

later at night we listened to the radio: london, belgrade, paris, and later to a long-enough broadcast in greek about the life of m. gandhi (on the hundredth anniversary of his birth). the cafe owner listened devoutly: said too (with authority) that gandhi had been the greatest public figure of our time. andreas listened too, quietly, jumping up only when it was over to see how the fish-lines he had cast in the water earlier in the evening were doing. (they were doing nothing.)

OCTOBER 6/69, FEAST OF ST THOMAS

the crowd got off for ikaria after all, all woke at four in the morning. wind was blowing strong but the captain had decided to leave in his little boat (and the harbormaster must have given him permission). his flock went with him: all but a few. one old fisherman said no: he'd been years on the sea and he wasn't going out on this one. the hotel owner, who's also a caïque captain, predicted they'd all be back in an hour. back or sunk was what he said. (now as the day ends all we know for sure is that they haven't come back.)

conversation of those who had stayed was loud in the lobby and i got up early to take a walk. as i came near the quay i heard a woman, laughing, it seemed to me at first, but as i got closer to where she was walking with the three sort of middle-aged men who were dressed for travel, i realized she was crying and quite hysterically. "manoula-mou" she said, "mama, mama, little mama!"—perhaps her mother had died in the night; but no. what had happened (whatever may have happened to her mother) was that the caïque had gone off without her, gone off without telling her it was going off; the captain who had a list of passengers apparently hadn't even called roll. worse, as the story developed, was that it had left her without a dekara (a thin greek coin with a hole in it that makes a penny look like a million dollars). the men listened solemnly as she talked and cried; i thought they might be her relatives.

i continued to walk up the dark road, past the awesome, apocalyptic rocks, under the very clear stars & took note (not at first but as the walk progressed) that the moon was in the last thin crescent of its cycle.

when i returned to the quay it was light and the woman was talking now to my friend the sponge captain: it was then that i overheard most of her story. the captain listened sympathetically, called the deserting captain a couple of rough kalymnian names, and predicted as everyone else had that they wouldn't get far in this weather anyway. "when the bay here is smooth as glass," he said, to make his point, "the ikarian pelagos has waves like mountains." what would it be like now. the woman, comforted by the captain's really sympathetic presence, but still, of course, in a plight, said she would go to the harbormaster's office when it opened, complain to him and ask for help.

sometime while it was still dark, i had gone to the cafeneion and drunk some tea with a paximadi (dry toasted bread crusts—a kind of rusk, good to dip in milk or tea), talked to three travellers: a father from samos who was bringing his son to school (to the theological semi-nary) here, and a boy from mytilini and samos. as we talked an older, bearded priest darted into the cafeneion for a minute. asked a ques-tion i didn't understand, got some sort of answer from the cafe-owner and left. then the owner, extracting what news he could from the action, explained to me that today was the feast of st thomas the apostle and that his liturgy would be held at the monastery on the hill, where they also have kept his head as a relic. what time would it be, i asked. they start early, early in the morning said the cafe-owner, but today maybe later. it will be from 7 to 10, said the boy from mytilini (black suit, white shirt, black tie, black straight shiny well-behaved hair, black-rimmed glasses, lively brown eyes; youth alone had kept him from wearing a theological beard).

(it must have been then that i took the walk and heard the lady crying.) i wondered if i would really go up to the monastery and listen to the liturgy. st thomas. (would merton be there?) i stopped by at a bakery and wished many happy returns of the day (a greek thing to do) to a baker-friend named thomas; as i left his place for another walk, i ran into my old friend siderako, the 88-year-old farmer who radiates joy (& gives it away) in his walk, and in every action. let's go to the church, he said, it's st thomas day. (his way of saying it could also mean, "i'm going to the church," there was no attempt, even hidden, to persuade.) but it was enough for me. "let's go," i said. he wasn't on his way to the monastery, as it turned out, but to a little (little, tiny) chapel of st thomas at the other side of the bay. we'd walk, he said (i'd heard of taking a boat). he had a walking stick, rare with him, but it was purely for show. i had (literally) a hard time keeping up with him as he swung along.

sometimes a scene, like the (sea-scape) from the road, is more alive and speaks more clearly than the imagination.

it speaks of amazing order and purpose.

islands set out with care & grace (as though for a tea ceremony).

rocks scattered helter-skelter on the hillside, as though after an explosion, as though after an apocalypse: yet each one "perfect" in its place.

a road that leads and bends, bends and runs straight in "just the right places."

(in just the right places.)

on days when nothing seems right in the world, the island landscape does. patmos does for patmos (& kalymnos for itself).

but patmos rocks are magical, mystical, holy.

the only ones like them i've ever seen, and they are only related in spirit, are those around avila.

they are rocks that stand and speak like elders.

some that rise from the sea are clenched like fists.

the rocks look like a person who has "suffered" a great revelation

like a prophet
after the spirit
has set him
free

even the brambles that grow from them, seem to be part, an essential part, of their visage

when i am alone on the road with the rocks, the whole world falls away, and i am alone & "contained" in a familiar place.

the color of the rocks is the color of fire (the color of pomegranates)

if a rock by the roadside is shaped for sitting, it is well-shaped for sitting (& well-placed, too, for meditation)

the rocks at patmos are vertical rocks; and the hill at patmos rises high

the holiness of patmos is priestly, prophetic, ecclesiastical holiness

the "holiness" of kalymnos is the holiness of life, of a city that is willing to live and willing to die: of one that praises its creator much as a fire does (by consuming itself in flame)

NOVEMBER 22/69   LIPSOI

it may be imagination, but i don't feel that the see oh pees are as happy to see me as they might be. not sure they'd be happy to see me in winter in any such isolated place. (only one of them anyway—a man who looks incurably human—has spoken to me with any warmth.) the others (this is not imagination) may even have been told to keep their distance, and even to keep their eyes wide open from there.

i haven't begun to discuss that part of the whole (or of almost the whole) mentality. the people i like to be with, the simplest, don't seem to suffer much from the dreams of alfred hitchcock. (but plenty of others do.) all kinds of intrigue, mostly involving shadows, seem to go on as regularly as bird-flight. and as a figure from outer space i obviously play an active role in many of these darkened imaginations. (they play a part in mine, too: though i try to keep their area to a minimum.) noticing them only if they notice me: treating them like a rash that would spread if given too much attention.

my fisherman friends seem really glad to see me: though all we can do is stand, or sit, around and smile at each other. it seems to be enough for them and is enough for me. they tell me, when they've seen me from a distance, too far away to have shouted from.

(but even that is one of the shadow-boys' complaints.) why should he hang around with fishermen? why not with respectable businessmen, doctors, priests or even postal clerks? do i imagine that this is what they wonder? no, i know it.

shadow-collectors delighted in half-moon flickerings of the new terrain.

a stunned metallurgic madman stared at the disappearing disc of sun.

indistinguishable, almost, from dark sea, the dark, dark figure who patrolled it.

a cross-eyed guardian checks the time of philosopher's night-walk.

metallic ear is nailed to the ceiling: records the pacings on the floor above.

a haiku (reduced to fourteen syllables) is locked in a trunk (which is locked in a trunk).

———

a man climbed to the top of a high mountain, walked to the precipitous edge of it and jumped off. "climbing to the top," he thought, "took considerable energy, and even walking across to the cliff took effort, but this descent," he said, "seems to take place without the slightest assistance from me."

the world, unified, had become one mind: the mind of one madman.

———

the city-planner has planned us a city

white as the disc of the hidden sun

silent avenues magically patrolled
houses of glass with see-through blinds
hours for work and hours for play
hours for defensive drill
& self interrogation

no mice, no rats, no cats, no dogs
no homeless men, no wandering clouds,
no vagrant thought

———

in mountains where sheep are
indistinguishable from snow
the snow from the cloud, the
clouds from the sky

an untutored clarinet
composes a threnody
for the atmosphere

names of the best known
boats have been embodied
in the song

which rises, reedy, to an
unseen listener
above the clouds, above the sky

———

trains arrive at the proper hours
& proceed to the wrong destination

endowments of perception locked
in a box while omens & prodigies
wander about

a gifted child is taught
to decipher the unwritten word

crossing Is & dismantling Ts,
inserting mythology in the
ellipses

ineffable distinctions to be
observed between first, second
& even third class derailment

———

the
strong
sun
works
the
fields
of
waves

———

does the grass
fear the dark

do the trees
fear the dark

does the sea
fear the dark

does the fish
fear the dark

does the grass
love the light

do the trees
love the light

does the fish
love the light

does the sea
love the light

―――

weary watch-dog
no special flock

barked at everything
that seemed
to wander

―――

(the tree claimed
the field to be its own:
granted licenses to birds;
allowed a certain number
of sheep to its shade)

(the grasses waved &
waved as the sun went
down: in a moment the
whole green valley would
be a jungle)

(the sea rippled. but
only slightly: was telling
its secret to no one)

the voices of the children
were strong as warriors: would
night subdue them one by one?

―――

the fly moves nervously outside the window-curtain, looking for a place of entry. manoeuvers, searches. seems to be tireless.

a zooming horsefly circles the room, swerves at the corners. (kalymnian boys on their motorcycles.)

a semi-hysterical hen or rooster calls as often as it breathes

all day all night all day all night, electric generator churns

a graceful slope of the hill, a non-committal bank of cloud. donkey-path, now a road, embraces the hillock

a winding road for a slow walk home

wide clouds fence in the pale blue sky: landscape is dim & dimly pensive

the hill is semi-permanent: the houses can be moved or changed

the sky seems solid, but changes lights & moods (& all behavior)

the whole of the day is obviously afloat: however great the vessel, it travels through a medium

we have been awakened to a ritual, a performance

light comes and stirs us, not to random movements: to something planned, to something long foreseen

will the baker do other than wake & bake?

the daily behavior is ground or base: particular actions can be altered

(on this particular moveable stage, these particular actors, acting)

through the fabric of it all, certain molecules were knitted: changing, rechanging, rechanging, changing

(the stage remained the same though every molecule within it altered)

the landscape was composed for the eye: the eye was prepared to receive its dispositions

as the traveller approached the island he could see the calm hills, the quiet houses, the broad, domed church that stood above the harbor the sweetness, the meekness of the island spoke to him, scarcely spoke to him

there had to be a certain truth in what he saw: whatever events might prove, there had to be some calmness here, some sweetness

to live was to be in motion: to move, in a certain sense, to live. not to change was not to be part of the fabric

(even dying was a kind of living) even as being born was

to change, to be in process. (was not so much important): it was essential

with each new revolution, the generator was exhausted and renewed

if spring in this moment graced the hills, would not a dry wind follow, and white sun later, and winter rains?

bird falls through the air toward a waiting tree

another sits and chirps in the rose-bush

lines of intelligence in the living air: the bird flies & cries

on a hill of white houses, one house of red stone

wind rising, the likelihood of high seas tomorrow

(an island has been known to disappear in a day)

the day was the common property of the people; the people, the common property of the day

waiting for nothing. hoping for nothing. expecting nothing. aware, nonetheless, of the change of light, the change of the seasons

on the west face of each house, the levelling light

the hills stand up to sing (an anthem of evening)

sun's formal fatherly leave-taking into the sea

last instructions: prescription for ritual of arising

(the quieter the land, the more apparent its rituals)

are we not to learn from the seasons; from season after season, to learn
& learn

in the earlier days no man could leave the island; we worked the fields
then, it was all we could do

———

(a man came from patmos—the barber tells me—and wanted me to
shave him. said i'd have to use hot water. i shaved him with cold. later
he went to the cafeneion and complained to the crowd. hot water?
said one of the men, we use that when we're going to slaughter a pig.)

———

michelangelo, leonardo, el greco . . .

lives of the artists . . .

troubled at first by the presence & meaning of a face he set out to
delineate . . .

saw in the faces of those around him meanings with which he was
already half-familiar . . .

could never have invented a human face. but knew with a line, with
a shadow, how to give it meaning . . .

one meaning or many meanings? there was really only one (mean-
ingful) face, & that was a face that searched for meaning . . .

one that searches
one that holds . . .

———

beauty without meaning
beauty without meaning;

beauty without grace
beauty without grace

———

a painting, a tent, a sail . . .

composed madonna; confident young man . . .

a cloud, with perfect composure, watches the hill . . .

the painting was a map, a compass & an arrival . . .

NOVEMBER 25/69

went last night to the cafeneion where manoli (diver) said he'd be. he
called me in to sit down for a coffee. why weren't you down at the
boat earlier, he asked with polite dismay: i'd have given you some
fusces (deep-sea shell-fish) for an appetizer. (i realized that if i'd wanted
fusces i should have been on the pier when the caïque came in.) i don't
really want them: but my landlady (fotini) would love some.

(& what fotini wants she usually gets.) she wants now, for example
(wants always), to go to kalymnos. suddenly her mother-in-law has
fallen ill and will be obliged to go (with fotini, of course) to kalymnos
for a check-up at the hospital (doctor's, local doctor's, orders). while
mother-in-law lies sighing in her bed, fotini dances in the kitchen as
though a prayer had been answered.

she has other ways of getting there, other pretexts: for example, her
teeth. each time a tooth troubles her she must go to the dentist in
kalymnos: and each time he sees her, he extracts a tooth. she loves to
visit the island, but will soon have no teeth at all.

solitude is all right (she tells me at breakfast) but one also needs ac-
tivity, a little excitement; one really needs both. & thus far, she's been
able to achieve the balance.

yesterday, too, involved some excitement. a woman from fourni, now
living here, had been having stomach trouble and treating it with
generous doses of new drugs (prescribed, no doubt, by the local doc-
tor): suddenly yesterday she began hemorrhaging and had to be taken
by caïque to leros (the nearest island whose hospital can be called a
going concern); fotini—a well-known good samaritan, & manoli (her
husband) & the local doctor went with her, taking her to the hospital
where she remains in doubtful condition (in need of blood which
hopefully some of the military posted there would be able to supply).
fotini, who'd gone in the kerchief, apron and bedroom-slippers she'd
been wearing when the emergency arose, saw friends she knew on

the streets of leros, and others, well-dressed people who were getting off the island steamer from kalymnos just as she passed: fotini was embarrassed by her own appearance, but had certainly managed to carry it off, and to be gracious to all she met. before returning with the caïque, the three samaritans stopped by for ouzo and bread and olives: the voyage home was over rough water, but the doctor, young, bright, bored, too, with life on the island, was now in good spirits and sang and danced a little for his friends. fotini returned to the house, tired, hungry, depressed doubtless by much that she'd seen, and yet exhilarated by the journey and by the feeling that she'd done what she should. "that's the christian life," she said to me, as i went off to bed.

———

night seems lighter, less heavy, here than in kalymnos, and considerably less heavy than in new york. the weight of people sitting around at night, the weight of their thoughts, the weight of their plans seems to create a physical pressure in the air above all the cities: creates, that is, a psychological pressure so strong that it seems tangible, physical, bears down like a weight on the shoulders.

it would be hard to imagine a similar weight bearing down on so small an island, being gathered even from the nocturnal fantasies (for so much of it rises from fantasies) of so small a community. perhaps it could. but just as new york seems heavier than kalymnos, and london perhaps even heavier than new york, the size itself of the city, and the number of perambulant dreamers within it seems to affect the magnitude of the weight that hangs above it and presses down.

for perhaps the same reason, an incident taking place (& i still mean at night) in the city has not the same weight as one taking place in a smaller town; an anecdote told at night in the city has not the same resonance as would have exactly the same anecdote told in an island village. there are paradoxes to be discerned here, because although life in a city seems to be constantly changing, each violent occurrence within it, each brutal fact, seems to be permanent, seems to be part of its unchanging face; in an island village the opposite is true: the hills about it are permanent, the seasons come and go in a stable rhythm; houses are built to stand till they fall; children carry the names of their forebears, and within this mostly comic framework, incidentals in the life of man seem smaller, more ephemeral: parts, rather, of a cosmic pattern than isolated omens of good or ill.

as a result, a country man takes news philosophically, whereas a city man is likely to hear it with panic.

_____

chinese literature (the novels, stories, & poetic dramas of sung & ming), though just as artificial as anything you can imagine, still holds us magnetized, because the fantasy of its authors springs from sources of real life (& real death). when blood is mentioned in one of these novels, it has the color and smell of real blood.

NOVEMBER/69

as a child (it seemed) he had played alone in the living room most of the time, dancing to records on the gramophone and performing in an imaginary theater.

(now it was only when he was quite alone that his imagination began to come alive.)

what he needed was not only quiet, but solitude: a solitude that honed itself against solitude.

the more he was alone, the more he lived in his imagination, the gaucher his outward appearance became. (he didn't mind this, particularly, but the community he lived in seemed to.) it is not that he doesn't shave, they would say, but his glances are not like the rest of ours: he seems to be looking somewhere else; it makes us, somehow, uneasy.

there was nothing they could, nothing they should even have wanted to accuse him of. (but his strangeness.) his strangeness, arising as it did from his own fantasy, seemed to awaken fantasies within them: they saw him in various roles (each according to his bent): some benign, some distinctly malevolent.

the police were really the least concerned with his actions or appearance: they had their own list of possible infringements on none of which he even approached to trespass: and so they went on playing checkers, and worried (if they did at all) about other matters.

arkheit (from his solitude) went on thinking benignly of all the inhabitants of the village. it was not his habitual attitude towards all creatures, but it had seemed to him (from the beginning) that this particular group of isolated beings was quite rare in the gentleness of its ways: quite lovable.

thus, if two women were talking as he went by, he would assume they were minding their own affairs. exchanging recipes, talking of their children, gossiping, even, but not about him. if the men looked up as he passed the coffeehouse, he knew it was a kind of shy greeting: he would look in, and say hello.

(they, in the meantime, were prodded by their demons: what would a spy be doing on our island? why should he come to trouble us, we who are so poor?)

––––––

i said to pandelis that nikita's children were nice and gentle and reflected what a nice guy nikita must be.

pandelis said: wait till you see my son, yanni. he'll be coming home soon from military service: then you'll see what a kid can be like. he's tall, good-looking, polite: has all the qualities.

a few days ago i was sitting with michali (antonia's—who'd finally come back from athens) in a cafeneion when pandelis went by. we called him in to sit down for an ouzo, and he said, with some excitement, that his son had come home. (he'd been with him just a moment ago, but didn't know where he'd gotten to now.) he stayed with us just a little while, then went in search of yanni.

several hours later, at night, around nine, as i came home from a walk i'd taken after supper, i saw pandelis standing outside of the cafeneion he usually goes to early in the evening. he was red-eyed, probably from ouzo, and looked tired.

where's your son, i asked him.

he's up at the other cafeneion on the hill, said pandelis, shall we go up and take a look at him?

sure: i said, let's go.

we'll just look in through the window, said pandelis as we started up the hill. it doesn't do to go in.

it doesn't? i asked (i half-remembered that it didn't).

no, said pandelis. father and son in the same cafeneion, it doesn't go: *einai tropi* (it's a shame, an embarrassment).

that's right, you're right, i said. that's a good rule. (it's an old one, too, i now remembered, in all parts of greece.) i wasn't eager, anyway, to sit around a cafe.

that's right, said pandelis. it wouldn't be right.

we got to the place, which was all full of kids, stood in the darkness outside and looked in through the window.

that's him, that's yanni, he said, pointing, it seemed toward a corner near the bar.

which one, i said.

that one, said pandelis, in the red pullover.

i still wasn't sure. one boy in a red pullover sat at a table in the corner. he was dark and didn't seem very tall. (he didn't look, either, as though he'd just breezed in from anywhere.)

the red pullover? i said.

yes, there!

now i saw the one he meant, in a red pullover all right, and standing at the bar. he was tall, good-looking and had the air about him you'd expect. he also looked like pandelis, at least, like pandelis' son. he was laughing with his friends, taller than they, not losing any of his bearing or reserve.

that's him, said pandelis, and after a moment: what do you say, shall we go in?

don't know, i said. i thought you said . . .

that's right, said pandelis, and we walked around for a moment in the nearby dark.

maybe i'd just ask him if he's ready to go home for supper, said pandelis.

sure, i said & (almost immediately) we started toward the lighted door.

oh, no, said pandelis, before we got there: he's sitting down with his friends now. he's starting to light a cigarette. it wouldn't do.

this time we turned around and left. went and stood for a moment on the wide terrace of the church overlooking the sea.

it's not right, said pandelis again, when he's in there with his friends. he may want to smoke (& he's not supposed to in front of me). they may have some conversation, some of it good, some of it bad. but i shouldn't be there to hear what they say, same with me. (a son shouldn't come into a cafeneion where his father is sitting with his friends, either.) just isn't right.

we started down the hill again toward pan's cafeneion.

i told him, he said, that if he wants to walk home and eat with me i'd wait for him here for a while. he said to wait if i wanted to, but he might be late. it's late now: must be after nine. i'll sit here a little while longer and see.

we went in and pandelis drank one ouzo slowly, and then one more. we listened to loud greek records on the juke-box. now we were both really ready to go: to leave the cafeneion at least, perhaps to go back up the hill again.

a young man, slightly older than yanni, came into the bar to play a record. pandelis recognized him, asked if he might have seen yanni.

he was up at the other cafeneion, said the boy, but he was just leaving when i came here.

pandelis got up quickly. he's left the bar, he said, let's go and see if we can find him.

back up the hill by another route we went: fast this time, and into a street that led to the same cafeneion.

there, leaning with one hand against a building, talking to a short, unshaven, fairly drunk-looking little old man in a mariner's cap, was yanni again, still bearing up well as a visiting prince, and pandelis was delighted to see him. the mariner was happy to see pandelis, too, took him off around the corner of the building and told him some kind of long story. i introduced myself to yanni & we talked.

when pandelis came back, he said, shall we go? yanni's reply was sort of a shrug. ok, he said. we all said good-bye. and they started together down the hill toward home.

(pandelis told me later (today) that yanni & his two friends had drunk twenty bottles of retsina amongst them that evening before they went home.)

FEBRUARY 25/70 (8.25 A.M.)

arrived yesterday morning early in high sea and storm; with me on boat new young police chief: civilian clothes but unmistakable characteristics. short-cropped black hair, clean short nose, eyes for squad drill; human qualities (existent, all right) tucked in like shirt-tails. universal navy-blue nylon trench-coat (cops & informers). sat near me on the boat at night but bored or upset by my mild conversation with home-coming seaman from leros moved off, later to shout a few pleasantries to wildly neurotic patmos girl returning (to patmos) from kalymnos clinic.

having shopped, gone for haircut, seen michali k, for a moment, returned to house, shopped again and returned again, i wait while rain falls outside the window for michali: may come by to take me to his house where his wife may have prepared a lunch we talked about yesterday: island lunch, seafood, something native, greek lipsiodic (lipsotic): maybe stuffed vine leaves: maybe boiled sea urchins. hope vine leaves.

again as before on the island a feeling of contrast, war even, between the real and the fantastic: everyday life and the life of dream; worst of everyday life, best of dream; best of daily life, blending somewhat with dream; worst of the daily, fused with the shadows of nightmare.

seeing through two lenses: one lens with a hairline split (like german camera) for greater accuracy: not a split like a broken pane, a broken mirror: but not (yet) the single vision of mystic or hasid.

what could be fuller of life than this (every) moment: each moment regarded calmly is like a jungle (or aquarium) bursting with life.

as jungle is full of beasts, so any moment is full (of many lives).

to look intently at any one object, may seem to leave the others out of account. but the attempt to look at all leaves nothing seen. (nothing regarded closely or understood.)

no problem solved by brutal decision to do either one or the other: to look at one thing at a time, or to attempt (even without recourse to seeing) to comprehend the whole.

no hope of comprehending the whole. no hope of understanding any one object, either, without some comprehension of the whole.

no hope of reaching a solution of these problems; no possibility of abandoning them, either (as long as one lives).

better to be engaged in them, be engaged by them, in spirit of play (serious spirit, serious play) while time passes over one, under one, through one.

SAME DAY/FOUR P.M.

three bad ways (bum circuits) of thought in the west bear the reasonably attractive names of chiliasm, angelism & quietism. the three, together and singly, are generally ill-thought-of by christian mystics & theologians.

if they exist as ways of thought at all in the east (& almost certainly the latter two do), they must have been given different names, and perhaps have had quite different careers.

chiliasm (coming from greek *xil*-root, meaning thousand) begins with the idea that the millennium (the golden age (?), the end of the world, the second coming, all at once) is about to dawn, and that, as a result, a number of restraints on human liberty which had prevailed up to now, should be abandoned, if only as a gesture of welcome for the time to come. among the first restraints (usually) to be abandoned by ardent chiliasts are clothing and sobriety. sitting quietly is not a chiliast

attitude: dancing is (mixed and naked): so are parades and demon-
strations (naked & mixed).

chiliasts have often been billy-clubbed & even shot down (in various
parts of the western world): angelists and quietists seldom run into
trouble with civilian law.

the fault of the angelist is to imagine himself more angel than man;
to identify himself (perhaps) with his own guardian angel, and to
imagine, not only that he must do no wrong, but that he can do none.

angelists usually live in monasteries, and, right or wrong, have sel-
dom gained the approval of their superiors here below.

the quietist does not believe that he is an angel, may not even believe
that he has one, he waits instead for direct inspiration (of the Holy
Spirit): waits and waits, doing as little as possible that might inter-
fere with his state of holy receptivity.

quietists, too, are often monks, and if they manage to fulfill their
monastic duties, are usually left to pray as they like. it is only when
they are moved to write quietist tracts that they find themselves in
trouble with the authorities. tracts then are usually written against
them (even bulls & encyclicals (?)), and their ideas declared, if not
heretical, at least out of bounds.

one feels that there is narrowness in the thought that condemns these
attitudes (all three) and that narrowness, perhaps, has had its day (a
long one) in the west, and could well be abandoned.

narrowness and neatness seem to go together in philosophic and theo-
logical thought, at least in the west: thought runs to systems: what-
ever doesn't fit the system must be considered heretical, out of bounds.

in the west, all things that are things are looked upon as "made-
things." example of made-thing: a box, a rabbit-hutch.

a box, almost any box, is the apparent result, at least, of all four
aristotelian causes: material, efficient, formal and final. it is made of
wood by a maker of wooden boxes, in the form of a box to be used as
a box.

on to tragedy. made of words by a maker of verbal tragedies, in the form of, and to be used as, tragedy.

what is the use of a tragedy? to cleanse the viewer of pity and fear.

on to civilization, the social structure, churches, the church, men, mankind, man.

on to music, the stars, the music of the stars.

whatever is a thing in the west is some kind of box.

naturally, including all natural things: trees, fish, cats, the sea.

these can all be understood through the four aristotelian causes. or if they cannot be so understood, the fault is more likely in the thing than in the causes.

an anomalous thing: a mysterious thing.

things in the west are made-things. even if they grow, having been "created," they are made-things.

even if they leap like athena full-blown from the mind of zeus, they are, from that moment on, to be seen as boxes.

———

in most western languages (would it be true in sanskrit, too?) "to do" and "to make" are one. (lat. *facere*, fr. *faire*.) no making without doing, of course: but no doing without making, either. to act is to make. (all action—at least in the west—some kind of making.)

all this (it occurs to me) may be a phase; an early, even primitive phase of thought: tectonic thinking.

(four phases discerned in the development of the arts by historian rudolph sommers: tectonic, naturalistic, decorative, selective.)

perhaps we haven't yet reached the naturalistic.

to come into being in the west is to be made ("i make a baby"): in the east it is to be born, to grow, to be pulled by the midwives of creation from pregnant "non-being" into visible existence (there to remain a while and thence to recede again into pregnant invisibility).

"coming into being and passing away" (aristotle called it "generation and corruption"), a natural enough kind of phase in the east, may sound to (the makers and breakers of) the west like euphemism.

FEBRUARY 26/70, 5 P.M.

a tragedy, or any other literary work, in the west will have a beginning, a middle and an end. (indian stories go on & on.) western musical works, whether symphony or opera, have beginnings and middles, and they leave you in no doubt about when the end has come: a crashing finale.

indian music starts as though from nowhere (as the casual result of tuning a sitar), rises to unpredictable heights (of anguish, joy, or meditation), descends again, and trickles off to nowhere. (you know it has ended when the last note is sounded and nothing, nothing follows.)

it has solved no problems: it has given no lasting insights. it is not likely, even, ever to be played again.

the instrument will be played again; the musician, too, may play again (molecules in both of them having changed): something abides; but not a frowning score.

———

I praise the Lord
for the beauty
of the sun

the beauty
of the sun

I praise the Lord
for the sound
of the wind

the sound
of the wind

the sound
of the wind

the beauty
of the sun

the beauty
of the sun

the sound
of the wind

the sound
of the wind

I praise the Lord

for the movement
of the trees

the movement
of the trees

the movement
of the trees

I praise the Lord

for the movement
of the trees

the sound
of the wind
the dancing
of the sun

———

in another
land

& with my
own compasses

I will not look
further for
righteousness